DISCIPLINES

OF THE

HOLY SPIRIT

1/27/01

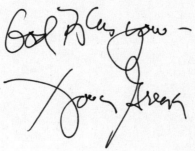

Bill

"In everything by prayer...
with thanks (phil 4:6)

God Bless you —

[signature]

DISCIPLINES

OF THE

HOLY SPIRIT

How to Connect to the Spirit's Power and Presence

DR. SIANG-YANG TAN & DR. DOUGLAS H. GREGG

ZondervanPublishingHouse

Grand Rapids, Michigan

A Division of HarperCollinsPublishers

Disciplines of the Holy Spirit
Copyright © 1997 by Siang-Yang Tan and Douglas H. Gregg

Requests for information should be addressed to:

ZondervanPublishingHouse
Grand Rapids, Michigan 49530

Library of Congress Cataloging-in-Publication Data

Tan, Siang-Yang, 1954–
　　Disciplines of the Holy Spirit : how to connect to the spirit's power and
presence / Siang-Yang Tan and Douglas H. Gregg.
　　　　p. cm.
　　Includes bibliographical references.
　　ISBN: 0-310-20515-8 (softcover)
　　1. Spiritual life–Christianity. 2. Holy Spirit. I. Gregg, Douglas H. II. Title.
BV4501.2.T255　1997
248.4—dc20　　　　　　　　　　　　　　　　　　　　　　　　96-46084
　　　　　　　　　　　　　　　　　　　　　　　　　　　　　　　CIP

Interior design by Sherri L. Hoffman

Printed in the United States of America

---

00 01 02 03 /❖ DH/ 10 9 8 7

Contents

Preface
Hungry for Spirituality

————•◦•————

Americans are on a search for spiritual reality. Local bookstores are overstocked with books, magazines, tapes, and other materials relating to New Age phenomena, mind-control techniques, self-realization strategies, Eastern mysticism, and other varieties of spiritual exploration. "Seven steps to eternal bliss" and "nine key insights into personal fulfillment" books promise to give one the secrets to inner peace, spiritual development, and relational success. But while the demand for spiritual food is an established fact, these materials will not satisfy the hunger.

This past year, nearly every major magazine has featured an article on God, prayer, angels, the search for the sacred, New Age phenomena, what people want out of church, and so on. Television talk show personality Oprah Winfrey recently featured a series "Does prayer work?" She sat in rapt attention during one session as Indian physician Deepak Chopra discoursed on Ayurvedic medicine, the spiritual life, life extension through meditation and exercise, and the elimination of toxic emotions. Overnight, sales of his book skyrocketed and within months passed the one million mark.

The search for spirituality has even made it to prime-time television. One show features two angels given assignments from God to either bring truth to someone's life or to show them they are on the wrong path, and, during a recent episode of the Emmy Award–winning series *Picket Fences*, disillusioned baby-boomer parents lack the confidence to teach their children about spiritual matters as their kids ask, "Is there a God?" and "How can I talk to him?"

In the midst of this search for spirituality, where is the Christian church and how is it doing? By and large the church has become conformed to the surrounding culture and no longer gives evidence in the life of its members to the teaching, lifestyle, ministry, and passion of Jesus. Our churches are filled with cultural Christians driven by materialistic values who are defining success in the world's terms. We have been seduced by media images of beauty, achievement, and power. Christians are no exceptions to the general tendency to seek instant gratification for different needs, including spiritual ones. We therefore have tended to seek shortcuts to achieving spiritual growth and have been left with a veneer of superficial spirituality.

Fortunately, more and more Christians, in recent years, seem to be dissatisfied with surface spirituality and are hungering for the depths of true Christian spirituality. More and more Christians are eager for a deep relationship to God that leads to a transformed lifestyle and spiritually empowered ministry.

We believe the deepest longing of the human heart can be met only through relationship to God—conformity of our hearts and minds to the life and character of Jesus Christ. This journey into true spirituality requires the transforming power of the Holy Spirit. We connect with the presence and power of the Spirit through the disciplines of the Spirit. As we intentionally engage in the spiritual disciplines, we put ourselves in places and situations where the Holy Spirit can do his transforming work. No one drifts casually into vital spirituality.

It is not our control and practice of the disciplines that makes a difference, but our yielding to the power and influence of the Holy Spirit through the practice of the disciplines that gives him space to speak to us and guide us, to fill us and empower us, to turn us around and transform us. We need to be yielding to the Spirit through the disciplines of solitude (solitude and silence, listening and guidance, prayer and intercession, study and meditation), the disciplines of surrender (repentance and confession, yielding and submission, fasting, and worship), and the disciplines of service (fellowship, simplicity, service, witness), in order to receive from the Holy Spirit the power to do what we cannot do on our own: love our enemies, live without unnecessary worry, and give generously of our resources. We have written this book to focus on the Holy Spirit's role in our journey toward true spirituality. We want to help Christians draw near to God in deeper love and intimacy, to know their identity in God through personal submission and surrender, and to be drawn into partnership with God in reaching a broken and lost world.

We are writing especially to those of you who are spiritually hungry and want a more vital Christian experience and practice in your lives. We want to reach, touch, and motivate you to pursue the true spiritual adventure of growing into the likeness of Jesus under the power of the Holy Spirit. Let's begin.

Acknowledgments

We dedicate this book to our wives, Angela Tan and Judy Gregg, for their loyal support and constant encouragement; and to our children, Carolyn and Andrew Tan, and John, Sarah, and Brian Gregg, who repeatedly remind us of the joys and blessings of life.

Our deep appreciation to Linda Rojas for her secretarial support, to Sandra VanderZicht and her associate Rachel Boers at Zondervan for their patience, persistence, and valuable editorial feedback, and to friends and colleagues Mike Flynn, Darrell Johnson, Katie Price Foster, and Cathy Schaller for their kind and helpful suggestions.

We are thankful to God for blessing us as we wrote, shared, and prayed together. May the Holy Spirit enable each reader of this book to experience his presence and transforming power, to the glory of God!

I

Connecting to the Power of the Holy Spirit

1

The Power of the Holy Spirit

———◆———

The world needs men and women fully alive who are growing into the love, character, and lifestyle of Jesus Christ. Such men and women are powerful testimonies to the power of God's living presence, his Holy Spirit. As we begin this book, we would like to share with you our experience of connecting to the power and presence of the Holy Spirit.

"Doug, do you want to be filled with the Holy Spirit?"

I (Doug) was raised in the Christian church, ordained into pastoral ministry at age twenty-five, and was "successful" in the world's terms for five years as an associate pastor in a large suburban church in Southern California. However, something was terribly wrong in my spiritual life: I had no personal prayer life, no sense of the authority of Scripture, no spiritual power or authority; further, my relationships were in a shambles and my marriage was in trouble.

Feeling burned out and ready for a change from the hectic pace of pastoral ministry, I seized an opportunity to return to graduate school and complete a Ph.D. in social ethics. Without realizing it, I was on my way out of the church and possibly out of active Christian involvement, abstaining from church attendance except for an occasional assignment as guest preacher.

In my mid-thirties, following graduate school, my family and I arrived at a small liberal arts college in Southern California where

I would be chaplain and assistant professor of religious studies. During my first year there I was attracted by the obvious love and spiritual vitality of some of the college students in the evangelical Christian fellowship. As I got to know these students better, I discovered they considered themselves to be "charismatics"—part of a renewal movement in their lives and in their churches through the power of the Holy Spirit.

This sent me on a search—through reading and conversations—to find out about the Holy Spirit. And that search led me to Marsha, an old friend in my former church, the chair of the social action committee, who, a few years before, had attended a catholic charismatic prayer meeting and been filled with the Holy Spirit. I was the first person she had told about her experience, and though I had listened politely, I thought at the time that she had gone over the edge and lost touch with reality.

I called Marsha and began asking her some of my carefully refined questions about the Holy Spirit. In the middle of our conversation, she paused and asked, "Doug, where are you right now?"

"I'm in my office at the college," I responded.

"Don't leave," she said. "I'll be right there."

This seemed a bit unusual to me because Marsha lived an hour away, but I now understand that the Holy Spirit was at work prompting Marsha to be obedient to a part she was to play in God's plans for me.

When Marsha arrived, we talked for another hour or so until I had come to the end of my questions, and then Marsha said, "Doug, do you want to be filled with the Holy Spirit?"

Well, why not? I thought. I was liberal, open-minded, and generally eager to try new things. But even more I was desperate, at the end of myself, and wanting to know if there was more to the Christian faith than I had previously experienced.

"Yes," I said to Marsha, "I want everything God has for me."

Marsha pulled a chair into the center of my office for me to sit in. Standing behind me and laying her hands on my head, she encouraged me to surrender to the Holy Spirit and ask for the Spirit's filling. "Ask and you will receive," she said. I prayed briefly, and then Marsha prayed at some length for God's promises to be fulfilled, for the Holy Spirit to come in power, for the gifts of the Spirit to be released, and for the fruit of the Spirit to manifest itself in my life.

"Well, what happened?" Marsha asked, at the close of the prayer time.

"Nothing," I responded, with some disappointment. I had read the book of Acts and its stories of the Spirit coming with power and had secretly expected that something of a dramatic nature should occur. But I didn't feel different at all.

"Let me tell you what happened to me as we prayed," Marsha exclaimed, as she shared visions of what she thought God was going to do for me and through me at the college. "God has great plans for you! Now that God has more room in your life, you'll begin to experience things differently and see him at work in your everyday life. I'll be praying for you. Expect great things to happen!"

I went home that day discouraged. But within days I became aware of a new excitement and joy in God. I was suddenly hungry to read the Bible—as though it was food for spiritual nourishment. Passages seemed to leap from the pages of the Bible into my mind and heart, bringing me under conviction about sin and God's purposes for my life. I began, for the first time in my life, to pray *and* listen, as though someone was in dialogue with me who truly cared. My prayers were simple and feeble, but the excitement of knowing God was truly real and present in my life, and that he could and would speak to me, was the "Good News" I so desperately needed. There were lots of fears too—that someone would find out what was happening to me, that I too had gone over the edge, that this new excitement wouldn't last. But through ups and downs, I realized that I was on a new journey, that I had turned a corner into a hopeful future, and though I was afraid, I wanted to go forward—I wanted more of God.

A few months later, during a weekend conference about the Holy Spirit, I felt drawn to ask someone to pray for me. When he asked what I wanted prayer about, I told him I didn't know.

We talked for a few minutes until suddenly, with a look of discernment, he said, "Doug, have you accepted Jesus into your life as your Lord and Savior?" I thought I had. I had been an ordained pastor for nearly ten years; surely I had said those words in my ordination vows. However, as his question penetrated my mind and heart that day I suddenly wasn't sure I truly had said yes to Jesus as both Lord and Savior.

"I don't know," I finally said to this stranger standing in front of me.

"Do you want to?" he asked.

I believe the Holy Spirit had been waiting for that question— a primary role of the Spirit is to point us toward Jesus, to draw us toward the truth of the gospel. I began to warm up from the bottom of my toes. I felt a rushing within me, warm and powerful, moving through my body and upward through my chest, uniting at some point with my spirit, causing me to say, in quite a loud voice, "YES!" I was surprised, even a little shocked, at my loud outburst, but I knew in that moment that I had been made for this, for intimate relationship with the living God. I was a bell being rung for the first time, finally aware of my true identity in Christ. Jesus, through the power of the eternal Spirit, had offered up himself to God so that I might be saved from sin and death and brought into relationship and service to the living God (Heb. 9:14). That day I said yes to Jesus, asking him to be my Lord and Savior once and for all.[1]

I have experienced the Spirit's filling many times since then— in the midst of an airplane trip, while praying for others, during preaching and teaching, in receiving words of knowledge, while operating in other gifts of the Spirit, in simple conversations with others, and after he has revealed to me something he is doing and invited me to partner with him in praying it into reality. I have come to believe, as does Siang-Yang, that we are to ask, and expect, that the Holy Spirit will fill us regularly, even daily, as we are surrendered to God's plans and purposes and ready to be obedient to his will.

The Spirit at Work in Siang-Yang

As a young teenager growing up in Singapore, I (Siang-Yang) searched restlessly for the meaning of life and an answer to my question of what happens after death. Two friends witnessed to me about Jesus Christ when I was thirteen years old, and shortly thereafter I asked Jesus into my life as my personal Lord and Savior. The Holy Spirit filled the empty void inside me with the peace and joy of the Lord. My fear of death was overcome and I received power in prayer and in preaching as well as boldness and effectiveness in witnessing and evangelism. In a one-month period during my first year as a Christian, I witnessed to one or two classmates a day, and twenty of my forty classmates accepted Jesus Christ as their personal Lord and Savior. I therefore experienced the Spirit's presence and power since I became a Christian in Singapore.

I came to Canada in 1973 to study at McGill University in Montreal. My family and I moved to California in 1985 from Toronto for me to teach at Fuller Seminary in Pasadena. My experience of the Holy Spirit's power and presence has deepened even more since attending a church retreat in 1989.

Since then, in the past few years I have been touched and filled with the Spirit during prayer, often with tears—tears of joy as I worship the Lord, as well as tears of compassion when interceding for others in need. On a few occasions—once when distributing the Communion elements in my church on a Sunday morning—I have even felt the compassionate heart of Jesus weeping for his people. And recently, while at meetings and conferences, I have felt shaking in my hands and arms as I stretch forth my hands to pray for people.

This shaking in my hands and arms also happened during my church's annual retreat for young adults as I prayed for one couple struggling with infertility problems. As I prayed, I experienced a boldness in faith and clear words from the Spirit that my prayer would be answered—that the woman would be pregnant and have her baby within one year's time, before the next year's retreat. The next year, just a couple of weeks before the annual retreat, a healthy baby boy was born to the couple. They laugh-ingly reported to everyone that it was my fault that they couldn't make it to the retreat. Young married couples at my church now tease me, saying, "Don't pray for us yet, Siang-Yang, we're not ready to have a baby!"

Being filled with the Spirit is a natural part of the believer's life, as natural as breathing. It is breathing the air of the kingdom of God. Each morning, I incorporate the disciplines of prayer, medi-tation, worship, surrender, solitude, Scripture reading, and listen-ing into my quiet time with God. These practices put me in touch with the transforming work of the Holy Spirit.

During my quiet time I usually confess my sins to God and ask for cleansing. I surrender my life to him, pray for the filling of the Holy Spirit, and ask for the Spirit to take control of my life and guide me. Surrender often turns to worship, sometimes accompa-nied by tears, and I experience the Holy Spirit's power along with a deep confidence and boldness at the throne of grace as I inter-cede for people. I read the Bible, paying attention to the guidance of the Spirit through the Word as I intercede for others and pray for deliverance, inner healing, growth, salvation, and transforma-tion. Sometimes these prayers are actually answered as I pray them, because the Lord is there, the power is present.

At the end of my time in prayer and meditation on God's Word, as I leave to go into my day, I pray for every aspect of my schedule—for the people I am meeting, clients I am seeing, and classes I am teaching. I commit every event of the day to the Lord and ask that all things be under his control. I thank the Holy Spirit again and say: "Fill me now and guide me through this whole day and make me your servant. Do with me what you will, and help me to grow and change into the likeness of Jesus. Speak to me about your will and purpose and use me to bring transformation into the lives of others." It is my desire to move from the solitude of the morning with Jesus into the activity of the day with him, by the Holy Spirit.

The Spirit-Filled Life

The Spirit-filled life is the Christ-directed life by which Jesus lives his life in and through us in the power of the Holy Spirit. Jesus promised his followers they would have powerful, loving, abundant, and fruitful lives as the result of being filled with the Holy Spirit. In the remainder of this chapter we want to share with you aspects of the Spirit-filled life and the blessings of being filled with the Spirit—but we especially want to tell you how you can enter into the loving and fruitful life that Jesus promises, and how you can experience the power of the Spirit in some of the ways we have described above. We want to encourage you to ask for and receive the same things from Jesus, by the Holy Spirit, that we have received.

First, we need to explain that a person initially becomes a Christian through the work of the Holy Spirit (John 3:1–8). From the moment of conversion, or spiritual birth, the Holy Spirit dwells in a person. In this sense, all Christians, at the point of conversion, receive "the baptism of the Holy Spirit," or as Paul says, we are all baptized by one Spirit into the body of Christ (1 Cor. 12:13). However, though the Spirit is present in all Christians, this does not mean all Christians are filled—empowered, released, guided, and controlled—by the Holy Spirit.

The filling of the Holy Spirit is an ongoing reality. Paul says in Ephesians 5:18, "Be filled with the Spirit." In the original language, this verse actually means "continually be filled with the Spirit." Renewal and a release of the Spirit's presence and power are needed on a daily basis.

Most of the time, the filling of the Spirit is experienced in a quiet way, with a deep sense of peace or joy, perhaps bringing clarity of insight or understanding regarding present circumstances or future plans. These times of filling may not involve intense emotions, and there may be a few days or weeks of "lag time," as was the case in Doug's initially asking to be filled with the Spirit, before it is apparent that the Spirit is at work in new ways. The book of Acts records a number of such instances where the manifestations of the Spirit's filling include boldness in preaching, greater wisdom and faith, and deeper joy (see Acts 4:8, 31; 6:3, 5; 11:24; 13:52).

Other times the filling of the Spirit happens with dramatic power and can include outward manifestations such as speaking in tongues, falling down, laughing, crying, shaking, feeling warm all over, or experiencing a power surge like electricity. Some of these outward signs are present when Siang-Yang prays for people for healing and deliverance. In the book of Acts there are four examples of dramatic manifestations accompanying the presence of the Spirit: with Jesus' disciples (Acts 2:1–4), with Samaritans (Acts 8:14–17), with Gentile "God-fearers" (Acts 10:44–47), and with Ephesian followers of John the Baptist (Acts 19:1–7). Some Christians refer to these four cases as examples of "baptism of the Holy Spirit" or "a second blessing," but we prefer to see these accounts as a special, dramatic filling of the Holy Spirit.

Dramatic manifestations in and of themselves are not necessarily signs of the Spirit's presence. God created us as unique personalities with different needs, so the Spirit touches us and empowers us in ways appropriate to our uniqueness. There is no such thing as a second-class Christian just because one does not speak in tongues or exhibit some other dramatic manifestation of the Spirit. What is most important is to be filled with the Spirit and to leave the manifestations to the sovereignty of God and the work of the Spirit.

The apostle Paul, who encourages us so strongly to be continually filled with the Spirit, also cautions us not to grieve the Holy Spirit, especially by sins of the flesh such as bitterness, rage and anger, brawling and slander, and every form of malice (Eph. 4:30); and not to quench the Spirit or put out the Spirit's fire by our unbelief and evil (1 Thess. 5:19). When we are open to the Spirit—continually filled and seeking to be filled—we are less likely to quench or grieve the Spirit in our daily living.

Blessings of Being Filled with the Holy Spirit

So why would you want to be filled with the Holy Spirit? Because you can't experience the powerful, loving, abundant, and fruitful life Jesus promises without him. Some of the blessings of the Spirit-filled life are:

- greater love and intimacy with God;
- exaltation of Jesus as Son of God and Savior;
- power and boldness to witness and preach;
- greater wisdom and faith;
- deep joy (singing and worship);
- release of spiritual gifts for ministry;
- victory over sin and temptation;
- effectiveness and power in prayer;
- quiet confidence during opposition;
- deeper trust in Scripture as the Word of God;
- renewed zeal for evangelism;
- fresh love of Christ and others.

The blessings of being filled with the Spirit are tremendous! That's why God tells us to be filled. He gives us the power we don't have, so that we can become more like Jesus and do the work of Jesus. All to the glory of God!

Steps to Being Filled with the Spirit

How then can one be filled with the Spirit? By asking! God is a good and generous Father who desires to give good gifts to his children.

First, confess your sins and receive God's cleansing and forgiveness by the blood of Christ (1 John 1:9). This step is essential because before we can be filled with the Holy Spirit, we must be emptied of things in our lives that grieve the Holy Spirit and displease God. Before we can be at home in God's love, we must realize that we are lost and in need of his mercy.

Jesus tells a story about a compassionate father and two lost sons (Luke 15:11–32). The younger son is lost because he uses his freedom to leave the father's house and make a mess of his life in a distant country, far away from the father's love and blessing. The older son, though he stays at home, is lost because he responds to his father out of duty, thinking he has to earn his father's love, thus missing out on the gracious blessing the father longs to bestow upon him. Henri Nouwen writes:

> I am constantly surprised at how I keep taking the gifts God has given me—my health, my intellectual and emotional gifts—and keep using them to impress people, receive affirmation and praise, and compete for rewards, instead of developing them for the glory of God. Yes, I often carry them off to a "distant country" and put them in the service of an exploiting world that does not know their true value. It's almost as though I want to prove to myself and to my world that I do not need God's love, that I can make a life on my own, that I want to be fully independent. . . . But the Father is always looking for me with outstretched arms to receive me back and whisper again in my ear: "You are my Beloved, on you my favor rests."[2]

We too are lost, needing to come to ourselves, to repent and confess our sins and return to the loving arms of our heavenly Father. The journey to our true home begins in confession.

Second, yield every area of your life to the control of the Holy Spirit, under the lordship of Jesus Christ (Rom. 12:1–2). We must give up the things we hold so close: known sin, anger, brokenness, rebellion, control, and pride so that God has authority over everything in our lives. "No one can serve two masters," Jesus says. "Either he will hate the one and love the other, or he will be devoted to the one and despise the other" (Matt. 6:24). No half measures. We must be wholeheartedly given over to God. C. S. Lewis puts it well:

> Christ says, "Give me All. I don't want so much of your time and so much of your money and so much of your work: I want You. I have not come to torment your natural self, but to kill it. No half-measures are any good. I don't want to cut off a branch here and a branch there, I want to have the whole tree down. Hand over the whole natural self, all the

desires which you think innocent as well as the ones you think wicked—the whole outfit. I will give you a new self instead. In fact, I will give you Myself: my own will shall become yours."[3]

Third, ask! In obedience to the command in Ephesians 5:18, ask to be filled with the Holy Spirit. God's purpose is to give you himself. "For everyone who asks receives," Jesus says. It is the will of our Father in heaven to "give the Holy Spirit to those who ask him" (Luke 11:10, 13).

Doug took a risk to say yes to the Holy Spirit and ask for the Spirit's filling and consequently began to experience a slow and steady transformation of every aspect of his life. He thanks God every day for the life God is pouring into him and through him to others. Siang-Yang experienced the power of the Holy Spirit early in his life, in the midst of preaching and evangelism and church leadership. Then, through some difficult "wilderness" times, he learned to depend more fully on God and to ask and expect that the Holy Spirit would fill and guide him on a daily basis. Both of our lives have changed dramatically as we have asked for, received, and been filled by the Holy Spirit.

As you ask for the Spirit's filling, pray specifically for his power and the release of his gifts so that you can live a more Christlike life and be more effective in building up the body of Christ and reaching out to a lost world with the gospel.

Fourth, give thanks. Thank God by faith for his answer to such prayers because they are in accordance with his will (1 John 5:14–15). Our prayers of thanksgiving acknowledge that God is present in everything he has given us—and he has given us everything. "Every breath we draw is a gift of His love," writes Thomas Merton:

> Every moment of existence is grace, for it brings with it immense graces from God. Gratitude therefore takes nothing for granted, is never unresponsive, is constantly awakening to new wonder and praise of the goodness of God. For the grateful person knows that God is good, not by hearsay but by experience. And that is what makes all the difference....

Gratitude is, therefore, the heart of the solitary life as it is the heart of the Christian life.[4]

We live in constant dependence upon the love and mercy of God, and our thanksgiving is a constant response to his help and guidance which comes to us at every moment through the power of the Holy Spirit.

Fifth, expect great things to happen. Anticipate that the Holy Spirit will work deeply and powerfully, whether in dramatic or in more quiet ways. Dwight L. Moody, the great revival preacher of the nineteenth century, was an ordinary man through whom God did something extraordinary. When Moody felt called by God to preach the gospel, he was a poorly educated shoe salesman with no visible signs of being a promising Christian leader. However, he was struck by a challenge from a friend that the world had yet to see what the Spirit can do with a person who is fully surrendered to God. While listening one day to the great preacher Charles Spurgeon, Moody was struck by the thought that the key was God in a person. Not a brilliant, or educated, or anything else kind of person. Just a person through whom God could work. Well, by the Holy Spirit, Moody thought, he would be one of those people. Sitting in the high gallery of Spurgeon's church, he thought, "It was not Mr. Spurgeon, after all, who was doing that work: it was God. And if God could use Mr. Spurgeon, why should He not use the rest of us, and why should we not all just lay ourselves at the Master's feet, and say to Him, 'Send me! Use me!'"[5]

You might say, "Well, I am not Dwight L. Moody, or Doug Gregg, or Siang-Yang Tan." That's right. You aren't supposed to be. God wants you to be you. He wants you to let him do through you whatever he purposes. He is able to do anything he pleases through any ordinary man or woman who is fully and wholly consecrated to him. If you feel weak, broken, limited, or ordinary, you are just the kind of person through whom God likes to work. The Bible is full of wonderful stories of God's mighty work through pretty ordinary people—just look at Jesus' disciples for the most obvious examples. Let God work with you in a powerful way— and expect great things!

Entering In

Do you want everything God has for you? Are you ready to be filled—empowered, released, guided, and controlled—by the Holy Spirit? Are you eager to experience the abundant and fruitful life that Jesus promised to each of his followers? If so, then you are ready!

Right now:

* Stop a minute and realize that your sincere desire to be filled, directed, empowered, and controlled by the Holy Spirit is itself the first step. Thank God that he has been at work to create this desire in you and that he is prepared to give you more of his Spirit as you ask, seek, and knock. (Luke 11:9–10; Matt. 5:6; John 7:37–39). Take a minute to review the steps outlined above on being filled with the Spirit.

* Now confess any sin that you are aware of, thank God that in Jesus he has forgiven all your sins, receive his promised forgiveness, and surrender every part of your life to God (Col. 2:13–15; 1 John 2:1–3; Heb. 10:1–17; Rom. 12:1–2).

* Ask to be filled with the Holy Spirit in obedience to his command to "be filled with the Spirit" (Eph. 5:18), and in trust of his promise that he will always answer when we pray according to his will (1 John 5;14–15).[6]

* Remember Doug's example. Don't be disappointed if nothing dramatic seems to happen. Expect that great things will happen, in God's timing. He knows you best—where you are and what you need and how best to

go to work to bring abundant blessing to you and through you to others. Remember Siang-Yang's example. Sometimes dramatic things will happen! Praise God for his work. Thank God for this great adventure in Christian living that he has called each of us into.

In the next few days:

Below is an example of the kind of prayer to pray on a daily basis. Let this be a beginning prayer for you each day for the next few weeks as you explore with us the disciplines of the Spirit and grow in your understanding and experience of the presence and power of the Holy Spirit in your life.

Dear Father, thank you for your love for me. I want to confess my sins to you as specifically as possible. [Take a few minutes, guided by the Spirit, to confess specific sins.]

I am sorry for grieving you. I know I have hurt you by doing things that are wrong and that displease you. I thank you that by the blood of Jesus Christ I can now receive your forgiveness and cleansing.

I want to yield to you every area of my life, including those areas where I might have strayed, and I do so now. [Again, take a few minutes, with the aid of the Spirit, to surrender anything in question.]

I pray, in the name of Jesus, that you will fill me with the presence and power of the Holy Spirit, that you will enable me today to become more like Jesus and to do what will glorify you, touch lives, and bring people closer to you. I commit to you all the events of this day. [Take a few minutes to list the events of your day.] *I ask that you will glorify yourself through me today and draw me closer to you.*

Thank you, Lord. In Jesus' name, Amen.

2

The Disciplines of
the Holy Spirit

N ow you know how to be filled with the Holy Spirit! In fact
you already are filled with the Spirit if you followed the
steps outlined in the previous chapter and prayed accordingly. "What's next?" you may be asking. "What do I do now?" The
short answer to your question, which we will be explaining more
in this chapter, is for you to connect continually with the Holy
Spirit through Spirit-given disciplines for the purpose of being
transformed by the Spirit into the likeness of Jesus Christ.

What God's Up To

God desires for you to walk in the Spirit day by day, year after
year, for a lifetime, in order to grow up into Christ. We are to be
built up "until we all reach unity in the faith and in the knowledge
of the Son of God and become mature, attaining to the whole
measure of the fullness of Christ" (Eph. 4:13, 15). God's very heartbeat, his deepest purpose, is that we "be conformed to the likeness
of his Son" (Rom. 8:29).

We can be converted to Christ in a moment, but growing up
into his likeness is the task of a lifetime. Yet this is our call—to
become "mature in Christ" (Col. 1:28 NRSV); to have the mind of
Christ in us (Phil. 2:5); to have Christ formed within us (Gal. 4:19
KJV). Conforming us to the image of the true Son is the deepest

work of the Holy Spirit. Our heart-longing and God's heart-desire meet as we give ourselves to his purpose of helping us become more like Jesus.

The apostle Paul's whole life's goal was to know—to fully and completely know—the Lord Jesus and to become more like him. Paul saw how glorious was the call and invitation into the heart of God—so glorious that he readily counted everything else he had going for him as so much garbage to be dumped into the trash in exchange for embracing and being embraced by Jesus. Paul wanted the righteousness that came from Christ, not some petty brand of righteousness that came from his own attempts to keep to a list of rules. He wanted to know Christ personally, to experience life in and through him. Paul saw and understood what God was up to, and he gave himself fully to this great adventure of becoming like Jesus. Writing from prison, near the end of his life, Paul could admonish us to learn from him, to put into practice the things we hear from him and see in him.

Like Paul, the apostle Peter saw and believed that we have been given everything we need for growth in godliness through our knowledge—our personal relationship—in Christ. Rooted by faith in God's love and purpose, Peter exhorts us to make every effort to add goodness, knowledge, self-control, perseverance, godliness, brotherly kindness, and love to our lives, "for if you possess these qualities in increasing measure, they will keep you from being ineffective and unproductive in your knowledge of our Lord Jesus Christ" (2 Peter 1:5–8).

Practice, imitate, learn from me, make every effort, Paul and Peter encourage us, for thereby we grow into maturity in Christ (1 Tim. 4:7). Dallas Willard, professor of philosophy at the University of Southern California, writes that "we can, through faith and grace, become like Christ by practicing the types of activities he engaged in, by arranging our whole lives around the activities he himself practiced in order to remain constantly at home in the fellowship of his Father."[1]

The Holy Spirit works in many ways over which we have little or no control to transform us into the likeness of Jesus—

through people we encounter, through circumstances, through our seeming failures, through daily trials and temptations. However, he primarily works in our lives by connecting us with his transforming power through the disciplines of the Spirit. Through the disciplines we surrender to the transforming process. We do have a measure of freedom in the disciplines, however. We can choose whether or not we will read the Scripture, spend time alone with God, and worship and praise him. By choosing to enter into the disciplines of the Holy Spirit, we are asking for more of God. We more often, more consistently, and more willingly put ourselves in a place, or into situations or contexts, where the Holy Spirit can and will shape us into the likeness of Jesus.

Let's summarize for a moment:

The goal: For us to become more like Jesus.

The Holy Spirit's part: He is the change agent, acting with power and purpose to grow us up into Christ.

Our part: We need to be changed, but we cannot change ourselves. We can, however, cooperate with the Holy Spirit in changing us by choosing to put ourselves in places and by staying put in places where the Holy Spirit can transform us.

The means: The disciplines are the conduits for the Holy Spirit's power, the God-given means we are to use in our Spirit-filled pursuit of growing into the heart of God.

Growing Into the Heart of God

When we are born again of the Spirit and enter relationship with the living God, the Spirit dwells in us. At this point of conversion, we are rooted in the heart of God—in the one in whom all things are possible. It is then that the Holy Spirit begins his powerful work of growing us into the likeness of Jesus.

This process of sanctification, of growing into Christ, takes place in three broad directions: The Holy Spirit works to (1) draw us near to God in deep love and intimacy, (2) help us surrender to his will and purpose, and to (3) reach out in compassionate ministry to others through us.

These three broad categories are well illustrated in the biblical story of the encounter of Zacchaeus, a hated chief tax collector, with Jesus (Luke 19:1–10). Zacchaeus had undoubtedly heard stories about Jesus, how he healed the sick and was willing to spend time with "unclean" people, sinners and tax collectors like himself. He wanted to see who Jesus was, so at some personal risk to himself he mingled with the crowds at a place where Jesus would pass by. Because he was so short, he climbed a tree to get a good view of what was happening. Zacchaeus was putting himself in a place where God would draw near.

When Jesus reached the spot from which Zacchaeus was watching, "Jesus looked up and said to him, 'Zacchaeus, come down at once. I must stay at your house today'" (v. 5). Everyone present began to mumble and complain because Jesus had spoken to this sinful tax collector and invited himself to dinner at his house. But Zacchaeus, overcome with awe and amazement that Jesus had received him and expressed love and friendship for him, came down from the tree and gladly welcomed Jesus to his house. Zacchaeus yielded to Jesus' loving invitation and, surrendering to him, put himself in a position of heartfelt confession and repentance.

During dinner, Zacchaeus called Jesus "Lord"—acknowledging his surrender to Jesus—and he promised: "Here and now I give half of what I own to those who are poor. And if I have cheated anybody out of anything, . . . I will pay back four times the amount" (v. 8). Zacchaeus's response of gratitude to Jesus that resulted in giving so freely of his possessions to the poor and his fourfold restoration to those he had cheated was far beyond the requirements of the law and cultural expectation. Now rooted in the love of Jesus, Zacchaeus's heart was transformed and he was prepared to reach out in love and service to others.

As a result of our encounter with Jesus (conversion), we too are drawn by his Spirit into deep intimacy, surrender, and compassionate ministry in his name (the process of sanctification, or growth, into God).

The Disciplines of the Holy Spirit

The disciplines of the Holy Spirit provide us with practical and realistic means of choosing to draw near, give up, and reach out. They are the means by which we become more like Jesus. They help us see how we can become, by the power of the Holy Spirit, an effective, love-filled community of believers growing into the heart of God.

The Holy Spirit draws us to God through three groups of disciplines: those of solitude, surrender, and service.

Drawing Near to God: Disciplines of Solitude

Solitude and silence establish and renew us in our relation to God. Through these disciplines the Holy Spirit works to transform us by drawing us close to God in intimacy and vulnerability, by giving us revelations of God's character and purpose, by speaking to us, and by strengthening us for battle.

Listening and guidance become vital practices as we grow to love and trust God. As we are drawn near to wait upon God, the Spirit may release words of knowledge and wisdom through Scripture verses, images, impressions, promptings, memories, or rememberings. We need discernment regarding what is received to ensure that it is really from the Spirit and consistent with the Bible's teaching.

Prayer and intercession draw us deeper into relation with God. As we enter times of prayer the Holy Spirit is at work to grow us up into Christ. In intercession we are close to the very heart of God, connected intimately with the Holy Spirit, who himself intercedes for us and others, articulating for us things too deep for words, revealing and interpreting the Father's heart to us. Through these disciplines, the Holy Spirit draws us into partnership in loving others, engaging in spiritual battle, and securing God's plans and purposes.

Study and meditation, especially of Scripture, brings us into intimate knowledge of God's character and purpose. Though the Holy Spirit can and will speak directly, he speaks primarily and most powerfully through the Word of God to draw us into knowledge of himself. We connect with the Spirit's power and hear his voice as we study the Bible. As we enter into the scriptural text and mull it over during times of meditation, we give the Spirit time and space to transform us through the Word, the "sword of the Spirit" (Eph. 6:17 RSV).

Yielding to God: Disciplines of Surrender

Repentance and confession strengthen God's authority in our lives. The Holy Spirit convicts the world of sin (John 16:8). As we reflect on our sin, taking time to be aware of our spiritual condition, the Holy Spirit begins a deep cleansing work within our hearts that brings us to repentance and confession. As we engage in these disciplines, we reestablish the Lordship of Christ in our hearts, so that the Holy Spirit can work through us to bring forgiveness and healing to ourselves and others.

Yielding and submission are active ways in which we willingly give up areas of our lives to the Holy Spirit's control under the Lordship of Christ. When the Spirit of God convicts us, and we repent and turn around, then we yield specific areas of our life to God. Examples of such areas include relationships, lusts, addictions, sins of the flesh, and other idolatries that hold us back from the fullness of the Spirit.

Fasting brings surrender of our appetites for food and other things we hold too close or take for granted (TV, music, recognition, money, relationships, travel). As we take a break or fast from things that "hold us," we give the Holy Spirit room to change us. He enables us to be appropriately disengaged from the world. He gives greater freedom from all the things that bombard our senses so that we can be more spiritually sensitive. He sets us free to experience more self-control and to take joy in our experience with God.

Worship is our deepest act of surrender to God. In worship, as the Holy Spirit helps us to focus on God instead of ourselves, we enter into intimacy with God in wholehearted submission. The Holy Spirit gives us fresh experiences of God's love and mercy, and we hear God's voice more clearly because our hearts are more finely tuned to him.

Reaching Out to Others: Disciplines of Service

Fellowship, gathering together in Christian community with other believers, connects us with the power of the Holy Spirit. As we share, worship, pray for healing and deliverance, receive guidance, support and help one another, extend forgiveness, and enter into confession and accountability, the Holy Spirit enables us to grow out of pride, jealousy, envy, competitiveness, selfishness, and all the other works of the flesh or sinful nature. He empowers us instead to grow in faith, hope, and love.

Simplicity is practicing a lifestyle that is increasingly free of excess, greed, covetousness, and other forms of dependence on the things of this world. The Holy Spirit works through simplicity to release spiritual gifts such as hospitality, mercy, and giving. He also empowers us to put first things first, to keep our eyes on God, to live free of anxiety, and to take better care of this earth.

Service connects us with the power of the Holy Spirit as we give ourselves to God and others in different ways. The Spirit empowers us as we exercise spiritual gifts for the building up of the body. The discipline of service constitutes a great adventure with the Holy Spirit—following his leading into costly service and sacrifice for the sake of Christ and his kingdom.

Witness, the power to evangelize unbelievers and bring them to Christ, also comes from the Holy Spirit (Acts 1:8). As we listen to and care for people, and are sacrificial with time, resources, and expertise in practicing the discipline of witness, the Spirit works through us to draw people to Jesus and the Father. We are invited into partnership with the Holy Spirit in his work of conversion and transformation of lives in the fulfillment of the Great Commission (Matt. 28:16–20).

The Role of the Disciplines in Human Transformation

We have given you a brief description of what we believe are the major disciplines of the Holy Spirit. The following chapters of this book will provide more detailed explanation. It should be noted, however, that we have not tried to give you an exhaustive list of spiritual practices. Keeping a journal, engaging in secret acts of kindness and other spiritual practices, though not given detailed treatment, will be mentioned along the way. Before we end this chapter, we would like to make a few more comments about the role of the disciplines in your spiritual journey.

First, while the disciplines are crucial means through which the Holy Spirit works and empowers us, they are not the only or exclusive means. For example, the Holy Spirit can begin to transform the life of a person who has not consciously entered into any Christian practices. We know of Muslims living in parts of the world still closed to the gospel who have been touched and converted by the Holy Spirit through revelation of Jesus in dreams and visions. God is sovereign over all things and can work in whatever ways and through whatever means he chooses. While he seems to work primarily through the disciplines, he can work apart from them.

Second, in and of themselves, the spiritual disciplines are nothing. Remember, they only help to connect us to the source of all spiritual power—the Holy Spirit himself. Without the Holy Spirit's ministry and enabling, the disciplines can deteriorate into legalistic practices that lead to spiritual death instead of spiritual fruitfulness. For years Doug took great pride in having a daily time of focused prayer and intercession. Gradually the Holy Spirit began to show him that his prayer time was largely a form of religious self-justification and performance before God rather than a time of listening and conversation with God. Doug learned that the disciplines are not a means of influencing God or winning his favor, but rather they are God's gifts to us through which he can minister his grace and mercy.

Third, God's power is made perfect in our weakness (2 Cor. 12:9). The path to power must always be the path of humble dependence on God. It is our desire that his transforming power touch the very depths of our being in order to ready us for ministry and service. Without Christ we can do nothing of spiritual significance regardless of our own energy, enthusiasm, or past experience.[2] The Spirit's power at work through the disciplines is not something we can grasp after, control, or "practice" into being. We must humbly enter the disciplines confident in God and not ourselves, ready for his power to be perfected in our weakness, remembering that human transformation is his work.

Fourth, God has given us more than one discipline because we need different practices at different times for spiritual growth. We are all unique persons with different temperaments, in various stages of spiritual development, for whom one or more of the disciplines will be critical in helping us grow in our relationship to God or strengthen that relationship where it is weak. Siang-Yang has been especially blessed in relationship with God through the discipline of study and meditation, while Doug has grown in the Spirit at key times through the spiritual practice of yielding and submission. And we both have a good friend who connects best with God through solitude and silence. As extroverts, we both know the danger of acting out of impulse and trusting in our own abilities, and have learned that we must set aside times for solitude, silence, and listening prayer if we are to be strengthened by God and directed according to his purposes.

The Heart of the Matter

The heart of the matter is the matter of the heart! This is especially true when it comes to spiritual practices. Our hearts must be fully involved if we are to avoid dead legalism, cheap grace, or superficial spirituality. We need to come to God with passionate desire to love him with all our heart, mind, soul, and strength. God has promised that we will find him when we seek him with all our heart (Jer. 29:13). As we seek him through the disciplines of the Holy Spirit, we will be found by him!

Growth in God requires passion, courage, persistence, patience, time, and self-discipline. Paul wrote to Timothy to remind him to "fan into flame the gift of God," which is the Spirit himself. "For God did not give us a spirit of timidity, but a spirit of power, of love and of self-discipline" (2 Tim. 1:6–7). We are not to be afraid or timid. That is not what God does in a life which has been filled by the Holy Spirit. Rather, he gives boldness and courage along with deep love and self-control.

The temptation to avoid suffering, to make excuses, to take the easy way out, to let someone else do the work, to play the victim, or to wallow in self-pity is always present. But this is not the way of Jesus. His way was marked by love, determination, patience, courage, and self-discipline. The same can and will be true for us as we enter into the disciplines, trusting the Holy Spirit's transforming work. Where the Spirit of God is present, there is always growth, healing, and new life. Where the Spirit is at work, there is always the possibility for courageous and self-disciplined living beyond what might be expected because of our past history or current circumstances. "Everything is possible for him who believes" (Mark 9:23).

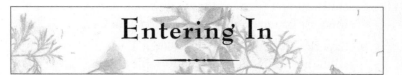

Entering In

Do you have a passionate desire to grow into the heart of God? Do you want to walk in the Spirit day by day, year by year, for a lifetime, growing in maturity in Christ? Do you desire to receive the transforming power of the Holy Spirit through the spiritual disciplines? If so, then determine now to seriously enter into the disciplines of the Holy Spirit!

Right now:

Spend a few moments in prayer. Ask God to fan into flame the gift that is within you. Ask that by the Holy Spirit your own spirit may be one of power, love, and self-discipline. Tell him that your will and heart's desire is to grow into the heart of God through the disciplines of the Holy Spirit. Ask him to give you courage for the days and weeks ahead.

In the next few days:

- Create a time schedule for reading the remainder of this book. We suggest you proceed slowly, taking time to absorb the material and experiment with the disciplines. You might want to read a chapter a week or every two weeks, perhaps as part of a small group, taking plenty of time to try one or more of the exercises suggested at the end of each chapter.

- Each of the disciplines is a way into the heart of God. No one of them is of greater value than another. Some of the disciplines will come more naturally to you. Take note and give special place to those disciplines that do come easily to you because they will be primary God-given ways for you to grow in relationship with God.

- Experiment with *all* the disciplines. Even the ones that seem most difficult or uncomfortable for you can bring hidden treasures of insight and revelation regarding yourself and God. Don't expect success or satisfaction with all the disciplines. If you do, you set yourself up for disappointment and self-condemnation. Determine to trust yourself with the Holy Spirit and enter this journey into the disciplines with eagerness for what God will reveal to you and what he will do to you and through you to others.

May God richly bless you in drawing near to him, yielding to his spirit, and reaching out to others.

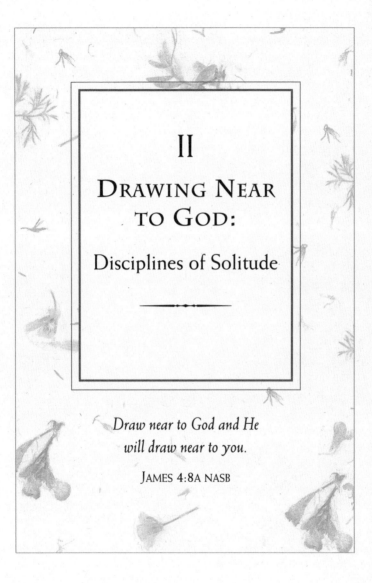

II

DRAWING NEAR
TO GOD:

Disciplines of Solitude

*Draw near to God and He
will draw near to you.*

JAMES 4:8A NASB

3

Solitude and Silence

———•◦•———

A few years ago Doug hurt his lower back at the very beginning of a family vacation in the mountains near Lake Tahoe. He was unable to follow his normal routine of leading family members on vigorous daily adventures of hiking, swimming, and exploring new places. At first he was sullen and depressed, and then angry, at his sudden loss of control. Where before he had been completely preoccupied with "doing"—creating meaning and purpose through planning a full agenda of exciting events—now he had to be content with "being"—moving slowly around a small mountain cabin, sitting up a few minutes for meals, lying in bed looking out a window, spending hours by himself.

Within a few days his mood began to change. Doug began to see God working through his forced isolation to draw him closer to God. The Holy Spirit had driven him into solitude, and the result was an opening to the strengthening presence of God. A bird's call, the rhythmic rocking of a lizard's head, the antics of chipmunks at play, the beauty of a single landscape—he suddenly had time to see and appreciate what was right outside his window. Doug realized that his lust to see a new landscape every day was just a reflection of the grasping, greedy, control-oriented, consumer culture that dominates our daily living. Because of his circumstances, he had time to see and receive. There was much more to be gained from solitude, silence, and quiet waiting than in all his striving—primarily God himself.

Solitude is being alone in purposeful withdrawal from human interaction. It is a deliberate choice to be alone in order to draw

41

closer to God by the power of the Holy Spirit, thereby freeing ourselves from bondage to people and things. Silence, the absence of speech, is a crucial component of solitude. While not all silence is solitude, silence is always a part of solitude. "Without solitude it is virtually impossible to live a spiritual life," writes Henri Nouwen.[1]

Solitude and silence are so transforming because they are essential ingredients and helpful preparation for all the other disciplines of the Spirit. Solitude is essential for Bible study, prayer, private worship, and journaling, and is common when fasting. Silence prepares us to hear God's voice and receive revelation and guidance.

The Holy Spirit Calls Us into Solitude and Silence

The Holy Spirit calls us, even "drives" us into solitude and silence, where we are strengthened in our relationship with God. "Jesus, full of the Holy Spirit, returned from the Jordan and was led by the Spirit in the wilderness" (Luke 4:1 RSV). During forty days of solitude and fasting, Jesus drew strength from his closeness to his Father as the Spirit prepared him to resist Satan's temptation of food, fame, and power. Again and again, solitary, desert, and mountain meetings with his Father became occasions for Jesus to be restored, renewed, and refilled with power (Mark 1:35; Luke 4:42; 5:16). Following such times of strengthening and refreshment in the presence of his Father, he had power to heal (Luke 5:17), he received discernment about God's will for choosing his disciples (Luke 6:12–16), and he conquered temptation in the garden of Gethsemane (Luke 22:39–46).

All of us have, at critical times, been "driven" into periods of isolation and weakness, where all the skills and abilities we had gained were seemingly useless for the tasks at hand, and we had to turn to God alone for resource, identity, and future direction. While painful at the time, these periods of solitude and reflection bring our relationship to God alive and prepare us for new seasons in which the Spirit becomes our teacher and partner in prayer and ministry.

All of us can expect, as Jesus did, that in times of solitude we will be established in our relationship with God, strengthened for spiritual battle, renewed in mind and spirit, and prepared for the plans and purposes God has for us. Jesus' exemplary life of intimacy, trust, and confidence in God the Father was born out of solitude. We must seek out times and places of solitude if we are to grow into the heart of God and become more like Jesus.

Being Prepared to Hear God's Voice

We live in a hustle-and-bustle world filled with all kinds of noise, sounds, and voices clamoring for our attention. We are constantly being bombarded by stimuli of all kinds, so that more often than not the still, small voice of God is drowned out. We complain that we do not hear God speaking to us today. The truth of the matter is rather that God is speaking, but we are not listening. To learn to listen we need to enter into the discipline of solitude.

We need to be quiet enough to follow the Spirit's lead into obedience, patience, humility, and all the other fruit of the Holy Spirit. We need to be alone enough to be weaned from the noise of life that crowds out spiritual growth. And we need to be alone long enough to become receptive of divine initiative and perceptive to God's "still small voice." God spoke to Elijah, not in the noise and drama of strong wind, earthquake, and fire, but in a gentle whisper in the midst of solitude and silence (1 Kings 19:11–13 KJV).

God speaks to the heart of those who keep silent in order to listen! In silence, we learn to control the tongue (James 1:26; 3:5–12). We don't need to say as much as we think we do. By giving up control of the tongue we learn to rely more on God's control. Silence prepares us for surrender and knowing our dependence on God. The less we speak, the more we see and hear. We become receptive to and perceptive of what God is saying and doing. We gain an increased capacity for discernment.

Sometimes it's when our lips are silent that we can really begin to hear others. When we choose not to exercise our right to speak, our minds and hearts don't have to be constantly formulating how to answer, explain, justify, or promote ourselves; we are free to just "be" in the presence of another and respond to their initiative. Because God is always taking the initiative in our lives, silence gives us an opportunity to hear what he wants to say to us through others. Believing that God is good, and that he will speak words of life and love to us through others, takes away the fear of being silent long enough to listen.

In Solitude We Grow in Intimacy with God

Today the heart of God is an open wound of love," writes Richard Foster. "He aches over our distance and preoccupation. He mourns that we do not draw near to him. He grieves that we have forgotten Him. He weeps over our obsession with muchness and manyness. He longs for our presence."[2]

We have been created by God for the deepest intimacy and fellowship with him. We are his bride, and he, as our Bridegroom, is the eager lover of our souls. He wants nothing more than to pour the fullness of his passion for us into the very core of our beings: "God has poured out his love into our hearts by the Holy Spirit, whom he has given us" (Rom. 5:5). The Holy Spirit is God's kiss to us, in which he fills us with his love and life. The fourteenth-century English monastic Julian of Norwich wrote of God's tender love with which he draws us to himself, comforting our souls and illuminating our hearts, making us "to love everything which he loves for love of him." In sweet companionship with Jesus we are lifted by his loving embrace and his gracious touch. "And when we are strengthened by his sweet working, when we willingly choose him by his grace, then we shall be his servants and his lovers, constantly and forever."[3]

For such deep and loving communion to happen, we must make time and space for God through solitude and silence, slowly creating inner and outer space that allows God's Spirit to become manifest to us. As we set our hearts on knowing and loving God, the worries, distractions, and temptations of the world are slowly dismantled. A new hunger makes itself known, the hunger for God's presence, for his love, for his life.

Growing up in Singapore, Siang-Yang would often go for long walks by the seashore. He would sit facing the ocean, watching the sunrise, reflecting on the beauty of God's creation and experiencing God's presence and love. Sometimes God's love was so tangible and real that he would cry with joy and gratitude. Wandering home renewed in spirit, he would spend more time in praise and prayer.

As we are faithful to the disciplines of solitude and silence, we grow in our hunger and thirst for God and his righteousness. And as we hunger and thirst for him, we are filled and satisfied (Matt. 5:6). Hunger for more of the Holy Spirit marks a person of God.

As we give ourselves to God in solitude, we find more and more that we do not want to miss our times alone with God. The more time we spend with God alone, the more we discover that God is with us at all times and in all places. Frank Laubach, an American missionary to the Philippines in the 1930s, set himself to the task of experiencing God in every waking moment of every day and discovered that this required two burning passions: "First, to be like Jesus. Second, to respond to God as a violin responds to the bow of the master."

During his daily walks up Signal Hill, on Mindanao Island, Dr. Laubach came to realize that "this oneness with God is the *most* normal condition one can have. It is what made Christ, Christ. It is what St. Augustine meant when he said 'Thou hast made us for Thyself, and our souls are restless until they find their rest in Thee.'"[4] Solitude is a primary means of hungering with our whole heart after God, and the fruit of solitude is growing intimacy with him.

God's Character and Purpose Revealed

King David, referred to in Scripture as "a man after [God's] own heart" (1 Sam 13:14; Acts 13:22), was, as a boy, shaped and tested in times of solitude. Tending his father's sheep, David had abundant space and time to grow in relationship to God. At night, when the sheep lay sleeping, David would gaze at the stars and strum upon his harp and sing the timeless songs of his forefathers' faith. He would break forth in abandoned praise, blessing the Lord with all his soul, with all that was within him, expressing deep emotions of joy, pain, gladness, and sorrow. David knew himself in relationship to God (see Psalm 23).

The apostle Paul, following his conversion on the road to Damascus, spent three years in the Arabian desert and many more years in isolation while God was preparing Paul for missionary work with the Gentiles (Gal. 1:15–18; 2:1–2, 8).

Siang-Yang now realizes it was during those periods of solitude he experienced as a teenager in Singapore that he first sensed God's calling to be his servant in ministry beyond the shores of his country. As God revealed himself to Siang-Yang and drew Siang-Yang to his love, he was already beckoning him to distant lands and quickening his spirit and mind to the Lord's larger purposes.

Strengthened for Spiritual Battle and Temptation

Jesus himself was led by the Holy Spirit into a period of solitude where he was tested in preparation for his public ministry. Satan appeared before him with three powerful temptations—the desire to be *relevant*, by turning stones into bread to feed the hungry masses; the desire to be *popular* and win approval, by leaping spectacularly and safely from the pinnacle of the temple; and the desire to be *powerful*, to rule the nations in return for worshiping Satan. Jesus responded to each temptation by quoting from Scripture in submission to his Father's purposes.

Christian leaders today are still tempted by the desire to be relevant, popular, and powerful: "Too often I looked at being relevant, popular, and powerful as ingredients of an effective ministry," writes Henri Nouwen. "The truth, however, is that these are not vocations but temptations."[5] The central question for us, says Nouwen, is will we be "truly men and women of God, people with an ardent desire to dwell in God's presence, to listen to God's voice, to look at God's beauty, to touch God's incarnate Word and to taste fully God's infinite goodness?"[6] Solitude and silence are the disciplines that draw us into God's presence to be strengthened in times of testing.

In solitude, we are purged of lusts and perverted desires and gain clearer perceptions of ourselves and others. The Holy Spirit is given time and space to speak to us, and we are given time and space to hear his voice. The Holy Spirit dwells in us, providing the power to overcome temptation and transform our testing, strengthening us for the battles ahead. We emerge out of times in solitude with a better understanding of our strengths and weaknesses and a deeper love and affection for God, our protector and defender.

When and how are we drawn, perhaps even driven, into times of solitude for testing and strengthening? Drawing near to God in solitude can happen when you have trouble sleeping at night or when you are led to wrestle with God in prayer regarding a decision to be made or the meaning of an event. Doug has learned to value circumstances that force him to be alone for a time: a lengthy car ride to a weekend conference, an uncrowded airplane, disrupted plans that strand him overnight in a strange city, laryngitis, or a severe flu bug. The Holy Spirit has worked in just these kinds of circumstances—when Doug has resisted the temptation to be angry and complaining because of his loss of control—to lead him away from temptations that were not obvious to him in the midst of a normal schedule. We cannot always choose the time and place of isolation and testing, but we *can* choose how to respond!

When we choose to engage in planned solitude, we have full assurance that God will draw near to us as we seek to draw near to him. Jesus said to his disciples: "Come with me . . . to a quiet place . . . to get some rest" (Mark 6:31). In rest, *with Jesus*, we regain perspective, are reminded who we are in God, and are made aware of the battle lines. The Holy Spirit will empower us through solitude to see the deceptions of the devil so clearly that they will no longer tempt us. Instead, we will see the eternal realities of God as so much better, more desirable, and worthy that we will have the will, desire, and power to choose God's path for us.

Dark Night of the Soul

Occasionally the Lord leads us into a time of isolation and solitude that can only be described, in the words of St. John of the Cross, as a "dark night of the soul." We may feel dry, in despair, or lost. God may seem absent, his voice silent. The prophet Isaiah declared, "Let him who walks in the dark, who has no light, trust in the name of the LORD and rely on his God" (Isa. 50:10). Such dark times can be pregnant with God's purpose; they can be times in which we are stripped of our overdependence on the emotional life, on the things of this world, and on ourselves. "The dark night" is one of the ways the Spirit slows our pace, even bringing us to a halt, so that he can work an inner transformation of the heart and soul. Those who are hungry for God can expect to be drawn or driven into times of dryness or confusion, where faith and dependence on God are tested and deepened.

A. W. Tozer describes this process as "the ministry of the night." In these times, God seems to be at work to take away from our hearts everything we love most. Everything we trust in seems lost to us. Our most precious treasures turn to piles of ashes. In times like these, says Tozer,

> Slowly you will discover God's love in your suffering. Your heart will begin to approve the whole thing. You will learn from yourself what all the schools in the world could not teach you—the healing action of faith without supporting pleasure. You will feel and understand the ministry of the night; its power to purify, to detach, to humble, to destroy the fear of death, and what is more important to you at the moment, the fear of life. And you will learn that sometimes pain can do what even joy cannot, such as exposing the vanity of earth's trifles and filling your heart with longing for the peace of heaven.[7]

As we seek to draw near to God, we can expect to have times in our lives when we too experience "the ministry of the night." Our best response during these seasons is to wait upon God, trust him, be still, and pray.

Entering In

Solitude and silence are an outward declaration of your inward hunger and desire to know God more fully and love him more deeply. These disciplines are critical for spiritual growth. They prepare you to really listen to God and receive his divine guidance. In solitude and silence you are drawing near to the God who "longs to be gracious to you." (Isa. 30:18). What an invitation! God waits for us to wait for him! Will you? Choose to connect with the love and power of God in solitude and silence, beginning today.

Right now:

Every journey begins with a single step. Get on your knees and ask God to help you to fight busyness, to draw you near to himself, to show you his love. Pray:

Lord, I can't do this myself. I need your help! I want to be near to you, to hear your voice, to grow in intimacy with you, to receive revelation of your character and purpose, to be strengthened to resist temptation, to be prepared for spiritual battle. Lord, show me what this means for me today and in the coming weeks. Reveal to me your plans for me to draw near to you in solitude and silence. I love you, Lord. Grow in me a hunger and desire for you. In Jesus' name, Amen.

In the coming days and weeks:

❧ Schedule time to be alone with God daily. If this is not a regular part of your life, you might want to begin with ten to fifteen minutes a day and try to increase the time to an hour a day. This daily time with God is probably the single most transforming experience you can under-take. It is the lifeblood of solitude and silence. To those who seek him regularly, the Holy Spirit gives himself in great abundance, bringing to them the most rapid, con-sistent, healthy growth in Christlikeness. Part of this time in solitude with God can include prayer and meditation on the Scriptures—we'll have more to say about this in coming chapters.

✤ Practice being silent perhaps up to a half or whole day. Make sure you explain what you are doing to your room-mates, spouse, or family! It takes time to enter into silence. Your first hour or so of silence may be characterized by many random thoughts. Living in an information-based society compels us to be constantly processing, and our minds are rarely quiet and still. It may take some time for your mind to slow down so you can be truly quiet and attentive to the Spirit within.

✤ Choose to listen to others around you before you speak. This involves consciously and continuously checking in with God before you respond, and deliberately evaluat-ing your intended speech to see if what you are about to say is really worth saying at all. By practicing silence this way in the midst of everyday life, you will come to real-ize that many of your words are only chaff. Silence gives the Holy Spirit an opportunity to sow his thoughts in your mind and heart!

✤ Take a half- to full-day private retreat spending time in solitude with God in a special or favorite place—at a local park, in nearby woods or hills, along the beach, or in a quiet, uninterrupted place in your own home. Don't over-structure the time. A long, leisurely walk in conversation with God, or reading and meditating on a few passages of Scripture, will be more centering and restorative than rac-ing through several chapters of Scripture or hurrying through devotional literature.

✤ Take longer retreats of 24 to 48 hours, or even up to a week, several times a year in order to draw near to God. You may want to go to a special retreat center for this purpose. The more you enter the rhythm of waiting on God, of giving him some of your best time, the more free you will be from pride and performance, the more willing to surrender false images of yourself.

4

Listening and Guidance

I n late March 1994, Siang-Yang attended the annual National Convention of the Christian Association for Psychological Studies, held in San Antonio, Texas. At the end of his workshop presentation, "The Holy Spirit and Counseling," which included discussion about the spiritual disciplines, he met an acquisitions editor from Zondervan who was very excited about the presentation and suggested Siang-Yang expand the material into a book, not just for counselors, but for the general Christian public. Siang-Yang was already convinced that the ministry and power of the Holy Spirit was crucial for counseling and other Christian ministries, and that he needed to teach, speak, and write about this more widely.

In prayer the next few weeks, he believed the Spirit was leading him to write the book, but that he needed a coauthor to bring additional ideas and perspective to make it a stronger book. In prayer, the thought came of approaching Doug Gregg, who had come to Fuller Seminary recently to serve as director of the office of Christian community, and who was scheduled to teach courses in Christian spirituality.

Meanwhile, Doug, being fairly new at Fuller Seminary, but with many years of pastoral experience and teaching in the areas of spiritual formation and spiritual renewal, was sensing the Holy Spirit prompting him, during times of prayer, to put some of his thoughts and experiences on prayer and spirituality into writing. He felt a kinship with Siang-Yang, who possessed a mutual interest in spiritual renewal, so it was with anticipation he met Siang-Yang for lunch on April 14, 1994. Doug was especially eager to share ideas he was having for writing a book about experiencing intimacy with God through listening prayer.

During lunch that day, Siang-Yang asked Doug what he was excited about writing. Doug began enthusiastically sharing his ideas about a possible book project. Then Siang-Yang shared his ideas, closing by asking Doug if he would be interested in writing a book together. While Siang-Yang was sharing, Doug experienced an inner conviction from the Holy Spirit that he was guiding him to work and write with Siang-Yang. And while Siang-Yang had already begun to think of Doug as a coauthor before their lunch together, he felt convicted in the midst of their conversation that God was leading him to write the book with Doug.

Both Doug and Siang-Yang realized independently that they had felt led by the Holy Spirit through Scripture and personal experience, and in the midst of their writing and speaking ministries, to focus more on the role of the Holy Spirit working through the spiritual disciplines to transform people into the likeness of Jesus. They prayed at the end of the meal for God to confirm this plan for coauthorship as his will and purpose, and within a few months, they submitted an initial proposal to Zondervan that eventually became this book: *Disciplines of the Holy Spirit*.

Created for a Listening Relationship

We have been created to be in a listening relationship to God. As we draw near to God, we begin to hear his voice and receive affirmation, encouragement, correction, and direction for our lives. Jesus says, "I am the good shepherd; I know my sheep and my sheep know me—just as the Father knows me and I know the Father—and I lay down my life for the sheep.... My sheep listen to my voice; I know them, and they follow me" (John 10:14–16, 27). We listen in order to receive guidance! The outcome of a close relationship with God is guidance and invitation into partnership with him.

Jesus didn't get up in the morning and say, "What great thing can I do for God today?" He said, "Father, what are *you* doing today? Show me what you are already doing so I can do it with you. I will do only what I see you doing" (see John 5:19, 30). Jesus' secret of guidance was his relationship of dependence on the Father—listening for God's voice, being observant of his Father's work, paying attention to his Father's leading in every circumstance of his life.

Do you believe God talks to people? That he wants to talk to you? Do you think it strange or unusual to hear his voice or to receive regular guidance and direction from him? Jesus believed that listening was fundamental to the Christian life and a natural consequence of deepening relationship with God. He encouraged believers that if they belonged to God, they should expect to hear from God. He rebuked the unbelieving religious leaders of his day, saying, "He who belongs to God hears what God says. The reason you do not hear is that you do not belong to God" (John 8:47).

As we draw near to the One who comes to us to draw us to himself, we enter into the disciplines of listening and guidance. We learn to hear the Shepherd's voice, to distinguish it from the many voices that compete for our attention, and to know and respond to his wooing and guidance.

The Work of the Spirit in Listening and Guidance

Hearing from God is the work of the Holy Spirit, who makes God's will clear to us as we engage in the discipline of listening and guidance. Jesus promised us his own guidance through the gift of the Holy Spirit. "The Counselor, the Holy Spirit, whom the Father will send in my name, will teach you all things and will remind you of everything I have said to you" (John 14:26). When the Spirit of truth comes, Jesus says, "He will guide you into all truth. He will not speak on his own; he will speak only what he hears, and he will tell you what is yet to come. He will bring glory to me by taking from what is mine and making it known to you" (John 16:13–14). The truth John speaks of here is not an idea, concept, or doctrine, but a true relationship. To be led into truth is to be led into the same relationship with Jesus that Jesus has with the Father.[1]

John speaks from his own experience as one who had heard, seen, looked at, and touched the "Word of life" (1 John 1:1). Thus, he could encourage those in danger of deception to depend only on the ministry of the Holy Spirit—"Christ's anointing"—for guidance: "The anointing you received from him remains in you, and you do not need anyone to teach you. But as his anointing teaches you about all things and as that anointing is real, not counterfeit— just as it has taught you, remain in him" (1 John 2:27). G. Campbell Morgan encourages us to wait for such guidance:

> To the individual believer, who is, by the very fact of relationship to Christ, indwelt by the Holy Spirit. . . . there is granted the direct impression of the Spirit of God on the spirit of man, imparting the knowledge of his will in matters of the smallest and greatest importance. This has to be sought and waited for.[2]

Paul, in his first letter to the Corinthians, emphasizes that it is the Holy Spirit who reveals the deep things of God to us. "We have not received the spirit of the world but the Spirit who is from God, that we may understand what God has freely given us" (1 Cor. 2:10, 12). We are so affected by our sin and rebellion that we cannot understand the things of God *unless* the Holy Spirit reveals it. He is our teacher. In reading the Scripture, we must sit before the Holy Spirit and respond to his leading. As we pray, we must expect that answers will come as the Holy Spirit guides us to Scripture, or through circumstances or wise counsel, or through personal words or a divine encounter.

Richard Foster writes that "In our day heaven and earth are on tiptoe waiting for the emerging of a Spirit-led, Spirit-intoxicated, Spirit-empowered people."[3] Such a people will not emerge, however, until there is a deeper and more profound knowledge that "in the power of the Spirit Jesus has come to guide His people Himself." We need, says Foster, an experience of his leading that is as profound and immediate as the cloud by day and the fire by night to the ancient Israelites.[4]

Our Part in Listening and Guidance

As you are becoming a Spirit-empowered person, entering into the experience of his leading, there are several things you can do to cooperate with the Holy Spirit in the process of listening and guidance.

- Let the Spirit build in you a desire to be yielded and obedient to God's will and plans. "To obey is better than sacrifice" (1 Sam. 15:22, see also Rom. 12:1–2; Ps. 81:11–13; John 14:21).
- Starting where you are, seek after God with your whole heart, striving to know him intimately. "You will seek me and find me when you seek me with all your heart" (Jer. 29:13).
- Resolve to want to glorify God and bring honor to his great name in all things in your life. "So whether you eat or drink or whatever you do, do it all for the glory of God" (1 Cor. 10:31).
- Be alert and sensitive at all times for the Spirit's promptings. Seek guidance from God; watch for it, expect it. Remember that the Holy Spirit is your teacher. "The Counselor, the Holy Spirit, whom the Father will send in my name, will teach you all things and will remind you of everything I have said to you" (John 14:26).
- Take time daily to listen and be in conversation with God. "Jesus often withdrew to lonely places and prayed" (Luke 5:16). Get into the habit of asking questions like, "What are you doing, Lord? What do you want me to see and understand in my current circumstances?" Keep a journal of such daily conversations with God.
- Wait for confirmation. "Test everything" (1 Thess. 5:21). God isn't in a hurry. Trust that he will confirm his will through Scripture, wise counsel, and circumstances.

- Take steps to respond obediently to the guidance you receive, trusting that God will provide confirmation and blessing. "Do not merely listen to the word, and so deceive yourselves. Do what it says" (James 1:22). "Faith by itself, if it is not accompanied by action, is dead" (James 2:17).

Means of Guidance

The Holy Spirit usually works through the following means of guidance:

The Bible, God's Word

God speaks primarily through his Word, as we read and meditate upon it. "All Scripture is God-breathed and is useful for teaching, rebuking, correcting and training in righteousness" (2 Tim. 3:16–17; see also John 14:26). In Psalm 119:105, we read, "Your word is a lamp unto my feet, and a light for my path." The Scripture is our standard of measure for all other forms of guidance. What the Spirit guides us into will always be consistent with the teaching of the Bible and will never contradict it. In addition, we must be careful to interpret the Bible accurately (see chapter six).

Prayer—Conversation with God

Prayer is not just talking *to* God, but dialogue *with* God. We listen for, and hear, God's voice in the midst of prayer. Paul challenges us to "pray in the Spirit on all occasions with all kinds of prayers and requests" (Eph. 6:18; James 1:5; Matt. 7:7–8; Phil. 4:6–7; see also chapter five).

Godly Counsel

Proverbs 15:22 says, "Plans fail for lack of counsel, but with many advisers they succeed." God often speaks to us through the wise counsel of mature Christian believers—pastors, church elders, leaders, spiritual directors, accountability partners—people who walk closely with God and who know him intimately.

Providential Circumstances

In Acts 8, we see how God used the providential circumstances of persecution and scattering of the early Christians throughout Judea and Samaria in order to spread the gospel (v. 1, 4–5). God can work through even our most difficult circumstances to guide us in a particular direction.

Sanctified Common Sense

As we think and engage in theological reflection, and weigh the pros and cons of options open to us, God works through our reason in bringing us to a decision. Even when it seems God has not spoken clearly, there may be times we have to choose an option because it is not possible to wait further. In such cases we need to use our best common sense to choose the alternative that will bring glory to God as the Holy Spirit leads us (1 Cor. 10:31).

Inner Witness and Peace

"Let the peace of Christ rule in your hearts" (Col. 3:15). Generally, the Holy Spirit confirms God's will to us by giving peace in our hearts. However, this does not mean we will always—or immediately—receive peace regarding God's guidance. There may be anguish or struggle, such as Jesus experienced in the Garden of Gethsemane in the process of obeying God's will to go to the cross and die for a sinful world (Mark 14:32–36; Luke 22:39–44). Jesus prayed and was obedient to God's leading, but experienced peace only later.

Prophecy and Words of Knowledge or Wisdom

"To one there is given through the Spirit the message of wisdom, to another the message of knowledge by means of the same Spirit ... to another prophecy" (1 Cor 12:8, 10). According to this passage, the Holy Spirit can guide us through words of knowledge (factual truth we did not know before) or wisdom (specific applications of God's Word or truth to a particular situation). Prophecy, on the other hand, refers to divinely anointed utterances given directly by God through a human messenger. Though there is some controversy regarding the exact interpretation of what Paul means by these phrases, we believe there are times when the Holy Spirit can and does speak to us directly with anointed and prophetic words, for example as the Spirit did in Acts 13:1–3. Such words generally come in the sense of a subjective inner voice, but at times they can seem to be audible words (1 Sam. 3:2–14). Some Christians are more comfortable speaking of these experiences as inner promptings of the Holy Spirit, rather than prophetic words.

Visions and Dreams

A mystery was revealed to Daniel in a vision (Dan. 2:19). The Lord called to Ananias in a vision (Acts 9:10–16). Both Peter and Paul were instructed by voices given in visions (Acts 10:9–23; 18:9–10). God has spoken to his people through visions and dreams in the past and we believe he continues to do so in the present.

Nature

"Since the creation of the world God's invisible qualities—his eternal power and divine nature—have been clearly seen, being understood from what has been made" (Rom. 1:20). God has revealed himself generally through nature and his creation. However, there are times when God touches us afresh and guides us through some part of the beauty of his creation—the grandeur of the stars on a clear night or the colors of a sunset. According to the psalmist, "The heavens declare the glory of God; the skies proclaim the work of his hands. Day after day they pour forth speech; night after night they display knowledge. There is no speech or language where their voice is not heard. Their voice goes out into all the earth, their words to the ends of the world" (Ps. 19:1–4).

Heavenly Visitation, or the "Hand of the Lord"

There are times when God reveals himself by an angel or special manifestation of himself. An angel of the Lord spoke to Philip

(Acts 8:26, 29). Jesus appeared to Paul on the road to Damascus (Acts 9:3–6). An angel appeared to Daniel (Dan. 9:20–23). "The Lord's hand was with them, and a great number of people believed and turned to the Lord" (Acts 11:21; see also Ezra 7:28).

This brief review of the means of guidance reminds us that we are meant to be in a listening relationship with God. We have been created to be, like Jesus, constantly aware of what God is doing. At any moment, anytime, day or night, in the midst of ministry or the most mundane tasks of living, God can and will speak to us. This is one of the most exciting elements of the Christian life. We are invited into a relationship of constant communion with Jesus through the Holy Spirit. "I am with you always," Jesus said (Matt. 28:20).

Increasingly Aware of God's Presence

Brother Lawrence, a seventeenth-century French monk, discovered that we can grow in listening and guidance until we are "practicing the presence of God," increasingly aware of his presence and gentle leading in all the circumstances of our living.

Missionary Frank Laubach set out to be consciously aware of God's presence for at least one second of every minute, beginning just one hour a day. He found that this made such a difference in his life that he could no longer imagine living in any other way.[5]

When Doug first read of Frank Laubach's experiments, he consciously tried to "practice the presence of God" on the way to church one morning—thanking God for law and order as he stopped at a stop sign, shooting "arrow prayers" toward people he passed, singing a song to Jesus in his mind. He found that he had never been better prepared for worship in his entire life. The whole service was radiant and filled with the presence of God. Doug was, for that hour, in Laubach's shoes, realizing that every day can be tingling with the joy of a glorious discovery.

That same week, as Doug took time one morning not just to talk *at* God, but to listen to him, Doug believes God said to him, "Go help your wife with the dishes." As he did so, God made it clear he wanted to draw Doug into deeper sensitivity to his wife, Judy, and into partnership with her in their home.

This kind of living does not happen effortlessly. We must desire it and seek it with all our hearts. It requires choosing a course of action that will draw us into constant communion with God. It means entering strongly into the disciplines of listening and guidance as a crucial means of experiencing deeper intimacy with God and receiving his transforming power. The results are staggering: listening becomes a launching pad for effective service and ministry in partnership with God; guidance brings confidence and peace that we are indeed in relationship with the living God; and hearing God's voice brings events of the Bible alive for us and allows our faith in the truth of the Word to rise beyond abstract conviction to heart knowledge of the truth.

Are you open to the various means of guidance? Do you expect God to speak to you and lead you as you take time to listen? Are you asking, as Jesus did, "Father, Spirit . . . what are *you* doing today? Show me what you are up to so I can do it with you!"

The Process of Guidance

As George Müller, a nineteenth-century English pastor, was reading Psalm 81 one day, he was convicted by the Spirit of the importance of listening to God. As he determined to listen and wait upon the Lord for direction, God began to guide and direct him in amazing ways. Müller began to live and minister completely through the contributions of people prompted by the Holy Spirit in answer to his prayer. By the time of his death, George Müller had been used by God to build orphanages that provided for over ten thousand children and had distributed over eight million dollars that had been given to him.[6]

Here's how Müller sums up the way he entered into a "heart" relationship with God and learned to hear and discern God's voice:

—I seek at the beginning to get my heart into such a state that it has no will of its own in regard to a given matter.

Nine-tenths of the trouble with people generally is just here. Nine-tenths of the difficulties are overcome when our hearts are ready to do the knowledge of what His will is.

—Having done this, I do not leave the result to feeling or simple impression. If so, I make myself liable to great delusions.

—I seek the Will of the Holy Spirit through, or in connection with, the Word of God. The Spirit and the Word must be combined. If I look to the Spirit alone without the Word, I lay myself open to great delusions also. If the Holy Ghost guides us at all, He will do it according to the Scriptures and never contrary to them.

—Next I take into account providential circumstances. These often plainly indicate God's will in connection with His Word and Spirit.

—I ask God in prayer to reveal His Will to me rightly and fully.

—Thus, (1) through prayer to God, (2) the study of the Word, and (3) reflection, I come to a deliberate judgment according to the best of my ability and knowledge, and if my mind is thus at peace, and continues so after two or three more petitions, I proceed accordingly.[7]

We open ourselves to mistakes if we allow the opinions of others to sway us from the clear instructions of Scripture, or if we are impatient in waiting for God's timing, or when our own wills are so strong we cannot get our hearts ready to respond to the guidance he gives. Guidance from God is seldom a simple occurrence; it is almost always a process of listening, testing, and discerning that leads to confident obedience. F. B. Meyer describes the process of guidance as follows:

God's impressions within and his words without are always corroborated by his providence around, and we should quietly wait until those three focus into one point . . . If you do not know what you ought to do, stand still until you do, and when the time comes for action, circumstances, like glow-worms, will sparkle along your path; and you will become so sure that you are right, when God's three witnesses concur, that you could not be surer though an angel beckoned you on.[8]

The Holy Spirit seldom uses all the means of guidance, but usually does bring several together in a process that brings conviction to an individual or group along with confidence to respond in obedience. In deciding to write this book, we were guided by the Spirit through listening prayer, circumstances, impressions, inner witness and peace, wise counsel, common sense, and a general conviction from the Word of God that we should write about the power and ministry of the Holy Spirit to a wider cross section of God's people.

Over lunch on April 14, 1994, the process of guidance became clear to us. "Circumstances, like glowworms," suddenly sparkled along our path toward a decision. We were filled with a sense of the Spirit's guidance—the hand of the Lord was with us, giving us the confidence to proceed in writing together. We were filled with the promise that God would be with us, driving us forward by a fresh wind of the Holy Spirit.

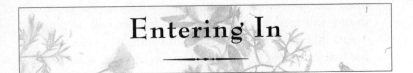

Entering In

Listening and guidance grow naturally out of intimacy with God. As we draw near, we begin to hear his voice and receive encouragement, correction, and direction for our lives. Ask yourself: "Am I looking to God, to my Good Shepherd, and following his voice? Am I eager to see what he is doing? Am I expectantly waiting for his guidance? Is my mouth, my heart, my life open wide to God?"

Right now:

Take a few moments to listen to God. Prepare your heart by turning any problems over to him. Remind yourself that receiving guidance from God is more his work than yours. Even though you don't have any great ability to hear from God, God knows you infinitely well and knows how to reveal his purposes and plans to you. Your part is to wait upon him and listen. Simply ask the Lord how he is praying for you, how he is at work in your life (Heb. 7:25; Rom. 8:34). Let thoughts come, and turn them into questions and conversation with God. Take note of any ideas, Scripture passages, or gentle promptings that come to your mind or spirit. Close by asking him to grow you in the practice of listening and hearing from him. As you leave this time of listening, expect to experience his guidance in the days ahead.

In the coming days and weeks:

� Set aside a few minutes each day this week to listen to God through his Word. Ask him to lead you to Scripture through which he wants to speak to your current circumstances. If you have a regular pattern of reading Scripture, ask him to impress upon your mind and spirit the meaning of a text and its application to your life. Pray with the psalmist: "Search me, O God, and know my heart; test me and know my anxious thoughts. See if there is any offensive way in me, and lead me in the way everlasting" (Ps. 139:23–24). Praying and listening through the Word will lead to praying about God's desires for your life.

❧ Set aside an hour or more one day, take pen and paper, and review the "Means of Guidance" section above. Write down examples of ways God has spoken to you and guided you in the past. As the Spirit guides you in this process, be strengthened in your confidence that God has spoken to you and that he will continue to do so.

❧ Experiment with practicing the presence of God. As Laubach suggests, try to be consciously aware of God's presence for at least one second of every minute for one hour a day. Jesus had an inward focus on observing God and doing only what the Father showed him (John 5:19). Commit yourself to doing the same. Be attentive to how God is working and speaking in all that is happening around you. Continually turn to God and ask what he wants you to be seeing, understanding, or doing. Keep a journal of what you are learning.

❧ As you intercede for others, do not assume you already know what to pray for. Take time to lift each person up to the throne of grace and ask God to show you how he is at work in their lives. Listen for the promptings of the Spirit for ways you can help, encourage, and meet needs.

❧ Gather with other Christians to wait upon the Lord, seeking God's mind about a matter of concern for your church or community. All promptings from the Spirit must be tested and confirmed by the Word, by circumstances, by inner conviction, and by the community of believers. Corporate listening is the best way to insure health and balance as you learn to listen and test the ways God speaks to you.

5

Prayer and Intercession

———————

P rayer is our primary pathway of relationship to God. It is an outward and visible sign of our inward hunger and thirst to know God more fully. David cries out, "O LORD, hear my prayer, listen to my cry. . . . I spread out my hands to you; my soul thirsts for you like a parched land" (Ps. 143:1, 6). "To be a Christian without prayer," said Martin Luther, "is no more possible than to be alive without breathing."[1]

Prayer is the oxygen of the spiritual life; without it, we die. When we are born from above by the Spirit of God, the life of the Son of God is born in us; we can either starve that life or nourish it. Prayer is the way the life of God is nourished in us. "Prayer," says Julian of Norwich, "unites the soul to God."[2]

Prayer is the central avenue the Holy Spirit uses to transform us. As we pray, we begin to see things from God's point of view and are drawn to pray according to his will and purpose. In chapter one, Doug shared how he prayed to be filled with the Holy Spirit, and how, as a result, God began to draw him near in love and trust so that he could receive Jesus as both Lord and Savior. Doug realized later that his prayers were themselves an answer to prayer. A small group of women at a Four-Square Gospel Church near the college where he served had been praying regularly for "the new chaplain" who was coming and continued praying for Doug by name every week during his first months in the job.

Doug was stunned to discover that people had been praying for him regularly during that most critical life-transforming stage of his life, and the Holy Spirit witnessed to his spirit that the intercession of those women had prepared the way for his transformation. During that time, he began to personally understand God's purpose and power through prayer. He started keeping a prayer journal that led directly to teaching others about prayer, which in turn has resulted in his present position as a teaching and training specialist with InterVarsity in the areas of prayer and spiritual formation.

Prayer is to be the main business of our lives. As we engage in the disciplines of prayer and intercession, we give God time and room to draw us near to himself and grow us into the likeness of Jesus.

The Work of the Spirit in Prayer and Intercession

Pray in the Spirit on all occasions, with all kinds of prayers and requests," Paul writes to the church at Ephesus (Eph. 6:18). The secret of prayer is found in those words, "in the Spirit." True prayer is in and from the Holy Spirit, breathed by the Holy Spirit. Spirit-breathed prayer brings us into the most intimate conversation and communion with God.

Through prayer, the Holy Spirit brings richness, vitality, and depth to all the other disciplines of the Holy Spirit. In the midst of solitude and silence we are drawn easily into prayer as God's love is poured "into our hearts by the Holy Spirit, whom he has given us" (Rom. 5:5). Often, during prayer, the Holy Spirit speaks to us and guides us, giving us direction for the future, as he did for Paul and Barnabas in Acts 13. And prayer flows naturally from study and meditation on God's Word. In this chapter, we will review some of the ways the Holy Spirit changes us through prayer by releasing spiritual power and spiritual gifts for the work and ministry we are to have in building up the body of Christ in love (Eph. 4:16).

To paraphrase the great preacher and apostle of prayer, E. M. Bounds, what we really need in the church today is people transformed by the Holy Spirit. We need more people who the Holy Spirit can use—people mighty in prayer. The Holy Spirit does not flow through methods, but through people. He does not arrive on structures, but on people. He does not anoint plans, but people—people of prayer.[3]

As we are being transformed into people of prayer by the Holy Spirit, we find there are many elements and aspects of prayer: prayers of adoration and praise, of confession and supplication, for healing and deliverance. A helpful aid, used by the Navigators and others, describes prayer as consisting of five parts, corresponding to the fingers of a hand: praise (for who God is), thanksgiving (for what God has done), confession (of our sin), petition (requests for ourselves), and intercession (praying for others). Let's take each of these five elements of prayer and see how the Holy Spirit works through them to bring us into deeper relationship to God.

First, the Holy Spirit helps us in our *praise* to God. "Praise the LORD, O my soul," cries the psalmist. "O LORD my God, you are very great; you are clothed with splendor and majesty" (Ps. 104:1). In times of praise, as our focus turns to God and away from ourselves, we "worship in spirit and in truth" (John 4:23–24). The Holy Spirit touches our spirits through praise and we are drawn into deeper union and communion with God (see chapter ten).

Second, in *thanksgiving*, we acknowledge that God is the great Giver and we are the recipients of his boundless grace and mercy. "In everything, by prayer ... with thanksgiving," Paul encourages, so our hearts and minds will be guarded by God's peace (Phil. 4:6–7). "Pray continually; give thanks in all circumstances" (1 Thess. 5:17–18). Through thanksgiving, the Spirit makes our hearts yielded, contented, and grateful.

Third, the Holy Spirit convicts us of sin and unbelief and leads us into *confession* and repentance for our refusal to accept Jesus and his message (John 16:8–9). The Spirit works through our confession to bring forth a fruitful, holy, and Christ-like life.

Fourth, as we *petition* God for our own needs, the Holy Spirit helps us to pray and even prays for us himself. "The Spirit helps us in our weakness. We do not know what we ought to pray for, but the Spirit himself intercedes for us with groans that words cannot express" (Rom. 8:26).

Finally, the Holy Spirit leads us in *intercession* for the deep needs of others. We are to pray in the Spirit at all times, making intercession for all the saints (Eph. 6:18). "The Spirit intercedes for the saints in accordance with God's will" (Rom. 8:27).

The presence and work of the Holy Spirit is crucial and central in praying. The letter of Jude directs us to build ourselves up in "holy faith and pray in the Holy Spirit" (v. 20). It is possible to pray in the flesh, "according to our passions," as James says (James 4:3), in which case prayer comes to nothing. Or we can pray according to the Spirit, setting our minds on the things of the Spirit. As prayer is guided by the Spirit and worked into us by his power, it will have its true effect. Wesley Duewel writes: "The Holy Spirit is the Spirit of prayer. He prays directly, speaking with the Father and the Son. He also prays indirectly, praying through you, the believer. . . . To be filled with the Spirit is to be filled with the Spirit of intercession."[4]

In the rest of this chapter, we will focus on ways the Holy Spirit works in our lives through petition and intercession in individual and corporate intercessory prayer as well as prayer in the midst of spiritual battle.

Individual Intercessory Prayer

Intercession, simply put, is praying for others—interceding with God on their behalf. Sometimes, the picture we present of intercession is of ourselves tapping on the shoulder of a very busy God who needs to be reminded of something important that he should do. We nudge him along by our prayers, telling him what to do, behaving as though the outcome depends on us. You might be laughing at this picture, but many sincere Christians pray in just this way, deciding what they want God to do and then persisting and prevailing in prayer to bend God's will to their own. Anger and disappointment often follow when answers to prayer don't come in the way they are expected.

A second, more accurate, picture of intercession is of waiting before God, developing quietness in the heart, listening for his still, small voice, so that God can tap *us* on the shoulder and get *our* attention. He invites us to partner with him in the things he is doing. Our part is to speak into being the things he is initiating. So, fundamentally, intercession is aligning ourselves—our prayers—with God's will and purpose. Jesus is, in this regard, our model intercessor, aligning himself perfectly with the Father in prayer: "I seek not my own will but the will of him who sent me. ... I always do what is pleasing to him" (John 5:30; 8:29 RSV). How thrilling it is, in the midst of prayer or even in the middle of the night or during busy activity, to be suddenly burdened with a need to pray for a friend or acquaintance. As Spirit-guided words tumble out of you with a life of their own, you pray for protection or wisdom for someone in circumstances you don't fully understand, only to confirm later that your intercession came at just the moment of crisis or danger in that person's life. When this happens, you know you have been in partnership with the Holy Spirit in accomplishing his purposes.

We know that God lives in us "by the Spirit he gave us" (1 John 3:24). As we draw near to God, having received the promised Holy Spirit, we will be filled with the Spirit of intercession. When the power of the Holy Spirit moves within our hearts, we must be ready to cry out to God on behalf of a person or situation.

When our intercession is in response to the Spirit's leading, it is backed up by Jesus himself. Paul says that "Christ Jesus, who died—more than that, who was raised to life—is at the right hand of God and is also interceding for us" (Rom. 8:34; see Heb. 7:25). Jesus tells the disciples in the Upper Room that when he leaves them to go to the Father, they will enter into a new dimension of relationship to him through the power of the Holy Spirit. Jesus promises to do what they ask in his name as they abide and remain in relationship with him: "If you remain in me and my words remain in you, ask whatever you wish, and it will be given you" (John 15:7). Our intercession is made possible, backed up, and given authority by Christ's continuing intercession. It is not our work, but God's work through us.

How do we move into intercession? Look for what God is doing right now. Realize that he has purposes and plans for each person for whom we are praying. Sometimes the Holy Spirit wants to show us the next step in a process of bringing healing or salvation to someone. Be in conversation with God. Ask questions like, "Lord, what are you up to? What is on your heart? How do you want me to pray for this person or this situation?" Then wait on the Spirit and cooperate as you are able in prayer and action. Give the Holy Spirit time to shape and direct your prayers. He will show you by words, thoughts, pictures, past experiences, Scripture verses, and other means that stir your spirit.

What can we do to become more open to the Holy Spirit's leading in intercessory prayer?

First, cultivate intimacy with Jesus. Draw near to God through the disciplines described in this section. Remember that the Holy Spirit flows through relationships, not methods; through people, not programs. We must stay close to Jesus; remain in him. Then acknowledge our dependence and ask for help.

Second, listen. When we develop a listening heart, we will become aware of what God is purposing. Listen especially to his voice through the Word of God and begin praying the prayers you find in Scripture. As this happens, we will develop a sense of what God wants to do in our lives. The words of the psalms are especially helpful and often give expression to the deepest feelings in our hearts.

Third, we must respond to the Spirit's initiative and invitation. We always have a choice to make when the Spirit prompts us to pray or gives us a burden for intercession. We can say no, and go on about our regular business. In the midst of hurried lives and a frantic culture in which busyness seems the most obvious virtue, the temptation is nearly always present to ignore or resist the Spirit's prompting. As we remain close to Jesus, however, and develop a listening heart, we will more and more often be able to say yes, and enter obediently into partnership with the Spirit.

In his daily prayer time, Siang-Yang intercedes for family members, friends, his church, pastors, leaders, colleagues at work, missionaries he and his family support, government leaders, patients and students he will be meeting with during the day, and other things the Spirit brings to mind. This is not a list he rattles through to fulfill an obligation to God, but the prayerful laying before God of his concerns for others, with the expectation that the Holy Spirit will be guiding his prayers. Doug often prays for individuals through particular passages of Scripture as he feels led by the Spirit. Since the Holy Spirit knows better than we do what to pray for, we generally lift up people and concerns to God and listen. Often he quickens our spirits to pray at length for a particular person or he directs us to pray about something that had not been on our minds as we began to pray.

The call to intercede can come slowly or quickly, and the time of prayer can last for a few minutes or an hour or two. Intercession usually involves a process that includes a time of preparation, or "birthing," that brings awareness of God's activity and anticipation of partnership with him, followed by a time of quickening and intensity in prayer. Prayer can include groaning or weeping and tears without words, because we may not know how or exactly what to pray. Finally, at the completion of an intercession there will often be a sense of release, accompanied by the deep peace of God.

Corporate Prayer and Intercession

We are in a better place to discern God's call to prayer when we gather together with other believers. Jesus said, "If two of you on earth agree about anything you ask for, it will be done for you by my Father in heaven. For where two or three come together in my name, there am I with them" (Matt. 18:19–20). Here is the assurance that when we gather together in Jesus' name he is present with us by his living Spirit. We will know his purpose and be able to pray with his authority.

The Holy Spirit works through the hearts and minds of gathered believers to provide checks and balances in the process of discerning God's will and to secure confirmation of the Spirit's leading through words of knowledge, revelation, and providential circumstances, bringing the gathered community to a heartfelt unity regarding prayer and action. In Acts 4, the gathered believers "raised their voices together in prayer to God," acknowledging the leading of the Holy Spirit in past and current circumstances, and asking God to enable them to speak about Jesus with "great boldness." After they prayed, their meeting house was shaken, "and they were all filled with the Holy Spirit and spoke the word of God boldly" (v. 24–31).

A few years ago Doug's church was facing several difficult problems—what to do with an earthquake damaged sanctuary, how to recover from sin patterns established by previous pastoral leadership, how to respond to a rapidly changing neighborhood, and what long-term direction to set for the church. The leaders of the church felt led by the Spirit to set aside a month for prayer and fasting to seek the Lord's face and know his will for the church. Teams of people were in the sanctuary night and day for that month, worshiping, waiting upon God, and interceding for the situations at hand. The Holy Spirit deepened their repentance and spoke through the Scripture, saying "Fear not . . . I love you. . . . Behold, I am doing a new thing" (Isa. 43:1, 4–5, 18–19 RSV). A wonderful rhythm with the heartbeat of the Father was established as they gained unity of heart regarding God's plans for the future. This time of listening prayer and discernment was the foundation for developing a long-range plan for the church that took the church deeper into their neighborhood and led to the formation of small group fellowships.

During the National Day of Prayer in May of 1995, the two of us gathered with others at Fuller Seminary for two hours of worship, prayer, and intercession. We sang and prayed that God would pour his mercy down upon us at Fuller Seminary; that he would humble our hearts and draw us close to himself, and cause us to cry out for our nation; that he would free us to become a people of prayer.

The Holy Spirit entered into our cries for the seminary, our community, and our land during those two hours. Convicted of his presence, we became houses of prayer as the Spirit poured his intercession through us and gave us boldness and authority to ask for his mercy and blessing on ourselves and others.

Jesus, referring to the Prophet Isaiah, declared that the temple in Jerusalem, God's house, would "be a house of prayer" (Luke 19:46; Isa. 56:7). He proceeded to cleanse the temple of those things that hindered right relationship to God. With the coming of the Holy Spirit, believers become God's houses. "Do you not know," says Paul, "that your body is a temple of the Holy Spirit, who is in you, whom you have received from God?" (1 Cor. 6:19). We are meant to be God's houses of prayer—established in intimate and dependent relationship to him, ready to be drawn by his Spirit into prayer and intercession.

Spiritual Warfare

Prayer and intercession also involve us in spiritual warfare. Appointing a time and place for prayer, getting to the place of prayer, and beginning to pray, is half the battle. Our flesh says, "I'm too busy, there are more important things to do." The devil says, "Why pray when you can plan, organize, work, hurry, and worry." Samuel Chadwick wrote, "The one concern of the devil is to keep Christians from praying. He fears nothing from prayerless studies, prayerless work and prayerless religion. He laughs at our toil, mocks at our wisdom, but trembles when we pray."[5] We need the Holy Spirit to draw us into prayer.

The other half of the battle is remaining in prayer. Resisting the temptation to fall asleep while praying, keeping one's mind from wandering, and avoiding unbelief and disenchantment when we don't see speedy answers to our prayers requires the discipline of the Holy Spirit. Jesus knew all about this. He urged his disciples "always to pray and not lose heart" (Luke 18:1 RSV). C. S. Lewis wrote, "The moment you wake up each morning, all your wishes and hopes for the day rush at you like wild animals. And the first job each morning consists in shoving it all back; in listening to that other voice, taking that other point of view, letting that other, larger, stronger, quieter life come flowing in."[6]

Entering into a life of prayer is entry into spiritual battle. God uses our prayers to invade enemy territory and establish his kingdom. As we are in tune with the Spirit, our prayers for others help bring physical, emotional, and spiritual healing as well as deliverance from demonic oppression. As Doug was praying for a friend suffering from severe headaches, he was led by the Spirit to see a deep pattern of worry, anxiety, and stress—especially around financial problems—that was gripping his friend. They talked about her anxiety and she felt convicted to ask God to forgive her for not trusting him for her financial future and for giving in to worry instead of trusting Jesus for her future.

As she received healing for these spiritual and emotional issues, Doug felt led by the Holy Spirit to take authority over the physical condition of her headaches—both their root cause and the persistent pain. As he did so, commanding them to be gone in the powerful name of Jesus, her headache disappeared. Wherever strongholds of sin exist in people's lives, or where emotional damage has created unhealthy patterns of defense or response, there is likely to be some oppression from the devil. When this is the case, the Holy Spirit will guide and use our prayers to take back ground lost to the enemy.[7]

Jesus spoke with authority against Satan's work, directly commanding unclean spirits to leave, lepers to be clean, the wind and waves to be still. Jesus effectively delegated authority in his name to others (Luke 9:1–2, 6). We can pray Spirit-guided prayers of petition and command because Jesus has gone to the Father (John 14:2) and sends the Holy Spirit to direct, teach, and empower us (John 16:13–15; see Luke 24:49; Acts 1:4–5, 8).

How do we engage in spiritual warfare? By listening to the Spirit and praying with boldness and authority as he gives prompting and direction. How do we go forward in battle? Through prayer and action, breaking all kinds of bondages and sicknesses of mind, body, emotion, and spirit—fevers, addictions, curses, inner vows of failure and self-hate, generational patterns of sin, and societal structures of evil and injustice.[8] We are to pray against every "mountain" that holds back our faith from receiving God's blessings (Mark 11:23–24), against all strongholds—"arguments and every pretension that sets itself up against the knowledge of God" (2 Cor. 10:5)—in order to bring every thought and action into obedience to the mind of Christ.

In the book of Ephesians, Paul confirms that Christ's heavenly position establishes authority for us (Eph. 1–2), which empowers us to wage spiritual warfare against all principalities and powers of this present darkness (Eph. 6). "For our struggle is not against flesh and blood, but against the rulers, against the authorities, against the powers of this dark world and against the spiritual forces of evil in the heavenly realms" (Eph. 6:12) We are to put on the armor of God so we will be strong in the Lord to take our stand against the devil's schemes. And having put on the armor, we are to "pray in the Spirit on all occasions with all kinds of prayers and requests" (Eph. 6:18), alert and persevering in our prayers for all the saints. Isaac the Syrian wrote:

> When the Spirit has come to reside in someone, that person cannot stop praying; for the Spirit prays without ceasing in him. No matter if he is asleep or awake, prayer is going on in his heart all the time. He may be eating or drinking, he may be resting or working—the incense of prayer will ascend spontaneously from his heart. The slightest stirring of his heart is like a voice which sings in silence and in secret to the Invisible.[9]

Entering In

"The great people of the earth today are the people who pray," says S. D. Gordon. "I do not mean those who talk about prayer; nor those who say they believe in prayer; but I mean those people who take time and pray."[10] Through prayer and intercession we build friendship with God, we put ourselves in a place to be transformed by the Holy Spirit, and we enter into partnership with Jesus in saving the lost, bringing healing to the sick, and delivering the captives. Do you want to be great in the Kingdom of God? Take time to pray!

Right now:

Ask God to grow you into a person of prayer. Acknowledge that you cannot really pray without the direction and energy of the Holy Spirit. Ask the Holy Spirit to be your teacher, strengthening you and guiding you into the where, when, and how of prayer. Take time to listen for his action plan. Remember that most Christians do not have significant lives of prayer, not because they don't want to, but because they don't plan to. Ask God to help you, to utterly control you by his Spirit. Believe by faith that he will, and thank him.

In the next few days:

✷ During this week, think of prayer as entering into friendship with God. Set time aside daily to deepen that friendship. Move through the steps of adoration, confession, thanksgiving, petition, and intercession. Make your prayers as specific as possible: "I thank you for_____; forgive me for_____." Spend time listening at each step, making your prayers a dialogue with God. Ask him to show you the tasks, blessings, and acts of love he has for you and others.

✤ Experiment with intercession. You might begin by praying for your enemies and for those who have mistreated you, as Jesus commands (Luke 6:28). This will get you started in a dynamic way that opens conversation with God and keeps you moving beyond superficial concerns into your own and the world's brokenness.

✤ Wait quietly and listen for God's leading. Let God bring to your mind any situations or persons for whom you should intercede. Lift these up before God, listening again for any special discernment or revelation that will guide the content of your prayers. Go to corporate worship a half hour early next Sunday and walk among the empty pews or chairs, praying for the people who will be sitting there during worship, expecting God to give you promptings and direction for your prayers.

✤ Join a prayer group at your church, or gather with a few others to begin a corporate time of prayer. Listen and intercede for pastors, leaders, members, and those God might be drawing to your church's ministry.

✤ Ask the Holy Spirit for an opportunity this week to pray with someone who is sick or facing some problem or struggle. Seize the opportunity when God presents it and enter into spiritual battle with the person through prayer. Ask God to release spiritual gifts of mercy, healing, and discernment in you and to grow you in confidence and experience in authoritative prayer.

✤ As you enter into the disciplines of prayer and intercession, keep a prayer journal of your interactions with the Holy Spirit. Record how God is at work in you to develop you as a person of prayer.

6

Study and Meditation

W̶e listen to God's voice primarily in the Bible, his inspired Word. The Bible establishes reality for us. Through study and meditation on it, we are given truth—truth about God's character and purpose, our brokenness and separation from him, his initiative in extending mercy and rescuing us through the death of Jesus, and his gift of a living Spirit to comfort and strengthen us in Christian living and to guide us into all truth.

Through study and meditation on Scripture we are powerfully strengthened in our practice of the disciplines of solitude and silence. We are drawn into solitude with Jesus as we begin praying the prayers of Scripture. Our ability to hear and discern his voice grows as we hear his voice in Scripture and test our hearing by the truth of the Word. If we would know God, and be growing into his heart, we must be intimately familiar with his Word.

God can and does speak to us through other means (see chapter four), but the Bible is his primary and central means of communication. All of our spiritual understanding and experience must finally be tested and confirmed by God's Word (2 Tim. 3:16). We can study and meditate on other things—for example, on God's character revealed in nature, or truth in Christian literature and art—but nothing we study will be of greater eternal significance to us than our study of God's Word. John Wesley, in the preface to his collected sermons, wrote:

> I want to know one thing—the way to heaven; how to land safe on that happy shore. God Himself has condescended to

teach the way; for this very end He came from heaven. He hath written it down in a book. O give me that book! At any price, give me the book of God! I have it: here is knowledge enough for me. Let me be *homo unius libri* [a man of one book].[1]

No habit is more invigorating for Christian living than regularly plunging into Scripture. No discipline provides more power and direction for spiritual growth than study and meditation on God's Word.

The Work of the Spirit Through God's Word

The Word is alive! The letter to the Hebrews tells us that "the word of God is living and active. Sharper than any double-edged sword, it penetrates even to dividing soul and spirit, joints and marrow; it judges the thoughts and attitudes of the heart" (Heb. 4:12). This "sword of the Spirit" is the only offensive weapon Paul lists as part of the Christian's armor. All the other pieces of armor are for defense against the powers of darkness. The Word of God, directed as a sword by the Holy Spirit, routs the enemy, bringing victory in spiritual warfare.

Jesus, resisting temptation in the wilderness, wields Scripture as a sword against the devil: "Man does not live on bread alone, but on every word that comes from the mouth of God" (Matt. 4:4). The emphasis here, as in Ephesians 6:17, is on a specific word from God as spoken by the Spirit through the mouth of a believer. Words of Scripture, supplied directly and immediately by the Holy Spirit—through prophecy or a word of knowledge or wisdom— becomes a sword which can reveal the secrets of our sinful hearts, break down the resistance of the nonbeliever, and even undo the work of the enemy when spoken against him in the authority of Christ and the power of the Holy Spirit.[2]

How important is it that we study, learn, meditate on, and know God's Word? As A. W. Tozer puts it:

Whatever keeps me from the Bible is my enemy, however harmless it may appear to be. Whatever engages my attention when I should be meditating on God and things eternal does injury to my soul. Let the cares of life crowd out the Scriptures from my mind and I have suffered loss where I can least afford it. Let me accept anything else instead of the Scriptures and I have been cheated and robbed to my eternal confusion."[3]

Study and meditation on the Word of God is truly a matter of spiritual life and death.

Below are just a few ways the Holy Spirit ministers life to us through the Word.

The Word Equips Us

Every part of Scripture is God-breathed and useful for teaching us truth, unmasking our rebellion, correcting our mistakes, and training us to live and serve in ways that are right and good and bring glory to God (see 2 Tim. 3:16–17).

During the past few months, Siang-Yang has been in a soul-searching process of understanding God's will for his future. The Holy Spirit has been guiding him, through the Scripture, to increase his time as senior preaching pastor at his church and to reduce his work at Fuller Seminary. The Spirit brought conviction to his heart through 2 Timothy 4:1–2: "I give you this charge: Preach the Word; be prepared in season and out of season; correct, rebuke and encourage—with great patience and careful instruction." Through these verses, the Lord reminded Siang-Yang of the gift of exhortation and preaching he had been given, and challenged him to give more of his time in exercising this gift for building up the body of Christ (Eph. 4:11–13).

The Word Cleanses Us

The disciples were cleansed and shaped by the words Jesus gave to them (John 15:3). "How can a young man keep his way pure?" cries the psalmist. He answers his own question: "By living according to your word," by "[hiding] your word in my heart that I might not sin against you" (Ps. 119:9, 11).

Several years ago Doug was led, through Paul's teaching in 2 Corinthians 10:3–5 regarding demolishing strongholds, to see a pattern of prayerlessness in his life. Habits, attitudes, and behaviors combined to form a stronghold set up "against the knowledge of God" (v. 5). Doug repented for tolerating this pattern of prayerlessness that was holding him back from growth in God and asked the Spirit to break the pattern and change his heart. Since that time, he has been more consistent and experienced greater joy in his prayer life.

As we study and meditate on Scripture, the Holy Spirit exposes our deepest motives (see Heb. 4:12). We see ourselves more for who we really are—"broken" people in need of God's mercy and transforming power. As we hide God's Word in our hearts, we are empowered by the Spirit to avoid sin and walk in Christ's victory.

The Word Feeds Us

We need to have regular, daily nourishment from God's Word if we are to live and grow spiritually (see 1 Peter 2:2; Heb. 5:12–13). George Müller was well known for his assertion that the vigor of a person's spiritual life was directly proportional to the place the Bible holds in that person's life and thoughts. Müller had read the Bible through a hundred times, always with increasing delight. He was greatly blessed by his diligent, daily study of God's Word, and counted it a lost day when he did not spend a good amount of time in the Scripture.

The Holy Spirit reveals "what God has prepared for those who love him" (1 Cor. 2:9), things we can never learn through scientific investigation. Apart from the help of God's Spirit, we cannot comprehend the thoughts of God and all the things that pertain to him.

The Word Guides and Leads Us

The Bible is a lamp to our feet, a light for our path (Ps. 119:105). The Holy Spirit works through Scripture to give guidance and confirming light and understanding regarding God's direction for our lives. In 1983, Siang-Yang was invited to teach and minister at Ontario Bible College in Toronto, leaving behind a more prestigious university hospital position. He and his wife, Angela, were quite happy in their current circumstances, and they knew this new position would involve both financial and professional sacrifice. Yet, through prayer and attention to God's voice in Scripture, they sensed the Holy Spirit calling them to this new ministry. They read, "Then the word of the LORD came to Elijah: 'Leave here, turn eastward and hide in the ravine of Kerith, east of the Jordan.' ... Then the word of the LORD came to him: 'Go at once'" (1 Kings 17:2–3, 8–9). The Spirit applied this passage of Scripture to Siang-Yang's heart, bringing with it a deep conviction that he and Angela should move eastward to Toronto, and that God would be with them.

While God does not always speak this specifically through the Scriptures when we have major decisions to make, daily immersion in God's Word puts us in the best place to receive both guidance and confirmation of his will for our lives.

The Word of God Produces and Deepens Our Faith

Faith comes by hearing the Word of God (Rom. 10:17). The Spirit uses the living and enduring Word as an imperishable spiritual seed to bring people to living faith in Christ (1 Peter 1:23). One of the best means of witnessing to unbelievers is to share the message of Christ through a judicious and sensitive use of appropriate passages from the Bible!

When Jesus was visiting with Martha and Mary (Luke 10:38–42), busy Martha complained to Jesus that her sister Mary was not helping with all the necessary preparations; instead, she was simply sitting at Jesus' feet and listening to what he said. "'Martha, Martha,' the Lord answered, 'you are worried and upset about many things, but only one thing is needed. Mary has chosen what is better, and it will not be taken away from her'" (Luke 10:41–42). Sitting at the Lord's feet and listening to his words is the one crucial, needful thing in all of our lives. In order for our faith to grow, we must take time to read and study his Word daily.

Getting into God's Word

There are many ways of drawing near to God in Scripture. We can hear the Word as it is read aloud, preached, and taught in church services, Sunday school classes, conferences or retreats, on radio or TV, on cassette tapes, CDs, or videotapes.

We can also read the Word. Blessed are those who read, hear, and "take to heart what is written," says John in the prologue to Revelation (Rev. 1:3). Reading three to four chapters of Scripture a day takes you through the whole Bible once, and the Psalms twice, in one year's time.[4] Reading the entire Bible ensures hearing the whole counsel of God (Acts 20:27).

The more focused effort of reading an entire book of the Bible in one sitting allows us to get the big picture of what God wants to say to us through the words of the original author. Doug received great personal and spiritual benefit from focused reading and re-reading of John's Gospel and Paul's letter to the Philippians. Getting the whole sense of what an author is saying through a book of the Bible decreases the risk of taking verses or portions of Scripture out of context and thus misunderstanding or misapplying God's Word.

In addition to hearing and reading the Word, we are also challenged to study it: "Do your best to present yourself to God as one approved, a workman who does not need to be ashamed and who correctly handles the word of truth" (2 Tim. 2:15). This requires regular study of the Word of God. The Christians in Berea were commended for searching the Scriptures daily to see if Paul was actually speaking God's truth to them (Acts 17:11).

There are many excellent Bible study aids available to help us in our "exegesis" (finding out what the text/passage originally meant) and "hermeneutics" (discovering not only what it originally meant, but what it means in today's context).[5] Ask, "What does the text say?" as you begin to study, seeking to find the facts, to know the truth. Then ask, "What does the text mean in its original context? What does the author intend for the first readers to know and understand?" And finally, "What does this text mean to me, for my church and community, and what must I believe and act on to be obedient to Christ?" At every point along the way, it is important to ask the Holy Spirit to guide us and speak to us through the study of God's Word.

Another important means of getting into God's Word and letting God's Word get into us is through memorizing Scripture. All the words of God's truth that we have hidden in our hearts will be there for the Holy Spirit to call to mind at a point of need for ourselves or others.

At one period in his life, Doug was struggling to understand and overcome frequent feelings of fear that were out of proportion to his actual circumstances. He recognized that his unreasonable fears were in part a sign of distrust in God, so he memorized a series of texts that gave him a Biblical perspective about fear, including, "For God did not give us a spirit of timidity, but a spirit of power, of love and of self-discipline" (2 Tim. 1:7). Doug meditated on this text and used it as a sword of the Spirit when fear came close. When he was in a situation that would cause him to begin to fear, the Holy Spirit brought this passage to his mind to warn him and strengthen him to resist the temptation. With this help, Doug was able to walk out of fear and into new patterns of boldness.

Siang-Yang has also made a practice of memorizing Scripture regularly, and continues to memorize two to three new verses from Scripture every month. This has been of tremendous benefit to him in his daily walk with Christ, as well as a great help in sermon preparation and ministry with people.

A note of caution: It is important to memorize verses in the context of the Bible passage or text from which they are taken, so that proof-texting, or taking verses out of context, can be avoided.

Meditating on God's Word

Without meditation, the ways for appropriating God's Word we've just described will be futile and unfruitful. Prayer, as well, can be empty and devoid of the Holy Spirit's power without meditation on the Bible.

George Müller made a significant discovery about the critical importance of meditation and the crucial connection between meditation and prayer that revolutionized his spiritual life.

> Now, I saw that the most important thing was to give myself to the reading of God's Word, and to meditation on it, that thus my heart might be comforted, encouraged, warmed, reproved, instructed, and that thus, by means of the Word of God, whilst meditating on it, my heart might be brought into experimental communion with the Lord. . . . Now what is food for the inner man? Not prayer, but the Word of God; and here again, not the simple reading of the Word of God, so that it only passes through our minds, just as water passes through a pipe, but considering what we read, pondering over it and applying it to our hearts.[6]

Meditation is pondering over Scripture verses or passages in such a way that the written Word of God becomes a living Word of God applied to our hearts by the Holy Spirit. The two primary words for meditation in the Bible mean "to murmur or mutter" and "to speak to one's self." Meditation is a process of thinking through language that takes place in the heart or inner life. The truth being meditated upon moves from the mouth (murmuring), to the mind (reflective thinking), and finally to the heart (outer action). The person meditating seeks to understand how to relate Biblical truth to life.[7]

This process is sometimes referred to as *lectio divina* (divine reading) where we listen to Scripture deeply with the ears of our hearts. We are like Elijah, listening for the still, small voice of God, the faint murmuring sound that is God's Word for us, the voice of the Holy Spirit touching our hearts. This gentle listening is an atunement to the presence of God in Scripture.[8] Once a word or a passage in the Bible speaks to us in a personal way, we can take it and begin to ponder it in our hearts, soaking ourselves in the passage. We can ask, "What is happening here? What are the sounds, smells, feelings? Why is God focusing me on this verse or idea? What does he want me to understand? Why do I need this word from God? How do I respond? Is there an example for me to follow, a sin to avoid, a command to obey, a promise to claim?"

In meditation, we seek to enter into the Scripture and live in it. We stand in the shoes of the disciples, alongside the Pharisees, in the kitchen with Martha, at the feet of Jesus with Mary. As St. Ignatius encourages us to do, we let all of our senses come into play. We see the friends lowering the paralytic through the roof. We smell the salt sea, feel the cool breeze on our face, and hear the lapping of waves along the shore of Galilee. We taste the bread multiplied by Jesus' hands as we sit among the crowd. As the Spirit works, we take time to meet Jesus in each passage, to have lunch with him, to address him and to be addressed by him, to touch the hem of his garment.

St. Ignatius, in his classic *Spiritual Exercises*, developed a month-long spiritual retreat centered around meditation exercises taken from the Gospels. Throughout the retreat we are to ask the Holy Spirit for special grace to bring about conformity to Christlikeness. During the first week, the retreat focuses on our sins as we seek the grace of receiving God's love and forgiveness. The second week centers on the life of Jesus and the need for the transforming power of the Holy Spirit to form us into the image of Christ. The third week addresses the suffering and death of Jesus as we ask for strength from the Spirit to die to our attachments to this world. The final week deals with the resurrection of our Lord as we seek the power of the Spirit to continually seek God and choose his ways.[9]

As we move from detached observation to active participation in the Scripture, our imaginations become active. Some have objected to using the imagination out of fear of its "subjective" focus and potential for self-deception or use by the enemy. But Jesus appealed to the imaginations of his listeners as he taught and told parables. While there is reason for caution and safeguards, we believe God can sanctify the imagination, just as he does our human reason, and work his good purposes through it.

Here are some simple steps we encourage for meditating or "living into Scripture":

1. Pray for the Holy Spirit to speak to you and guide you as you read a passage of Scripture.
2. Read through the passage you are meditating on several times, listening for the still, small voice of God and waiting upon the leading of the Spirit.
3. Ponder the verse or two that grabs your attention or touches you in some way. Picture what is happening as though you are behind the lens of a camera looking at the scene, for example, Jesus' feeding the five thousand with five loaves and two fish. See the little boy give his lunch to Jesus. Picture and hear Jesus' conversation with the disciples.
4. Come out from behind the camera and put yourself in the picture—in Jesus' shoes, or in the shoes of the disciples or the people gathered around. Ask questions. What is Jesus thinking? Why is he acting in this way? Allow a dialogue to unfold inside of you; let your imagination and senses be instruments for revelation from the Holy Spirit.
5. Be open to the ways God may want to speak to you directly through his Word: through a personal encounter, as you stand alongside one of the disciples; as you ask questions; perhaps as Jesus comes directly to you in the scene in which you have entered.
6. Write down what you have heard from God or what you have learned through your meditation on his Word.
7. Take time to share what God has said to you with an accountability partner or wise friend. This provides protection by checking what comes from your time of meditation, helps to reinforce God's Word to you, and encourages and blesses others in their journey of faith.

Let's summarize by sharing a simple way of remembering how to get into God's Word. Look at your hand. Think of hearing, reading, studying, and memorizing representing the first four fingers of your hand, with meditating as the thumb that touches the other fingers.[10] By these means, the Holy Spirit can speak the living Word of God to your heart. The Holy Spirit is the one who enables us to understand the thoughts and things of God. Without his ministry as teacher of truth and revealer of God's mind and heart to us, we will not be able to know or understand God or spiritual things (see 1 Cor. 2:6–16). With this in mind, always begin your reading, study, and meditation by asking for the Spirit's illumination and guidance, and throughout the process of getting into God's Word, be sensitive to his voice speaking to you!

Entering In

Jesus reminds us that heaven and earth will pass away, but his words will never pass away (Matt. 24:35). God's Word is absolutely trustworthy; it is eternal and endures forever (Isa. 40:8). Paul exhorts us to let the Word of Christ dwell in us richly as we teach and admonish one another with all wisdom, and sing psalms, hymns, and spiritual songs with gratitude in our hearts to God (Col. 3:16). Let us more and more, each and every day, be a people of the Word, growing into the image of Christ as we draw near to God through study and meditation.

Right now:

Read 2 Timothy 3:16. Ask the Holy Spirit to speak to you and empower you through the Word of God, which is the sword of the Spirit (Eph. 6:17). Ask God to help you become a person of the Word!

In the coming days and weeks:

✾ Decide to read the Bible on a daily basis. Start by reading a chapter a day, pausing to meditate on a verse or two that the Spirit brings to your attention. Review the steps of meditation. Ask questions of the text and enter into dialogue with the Spirit as you ruminate on the Word. If you are more ambitious, you may want to pick up a copy of *The One Year Bible* published by Tyndale and read the three or four chapters assigned daily so that you can read through the whole Bible in one year.

❦ Combine your Bible reading and meditation time with your prayer time. Remember what George Müller learned—meditation and prayer are crucial means of knowing God and the Holy Spirit's power.

❦ Make a commitment to memorize at least one verse or text of Scripture a month. If you haven't already done so, try the *Topical Memory System* put out by the Navigators. It should be available at your local Christian bookstore.

❦ The study of God's Word requires discipline—which includes careful thought, reflection, and reading of Bible study aids or tools like commentaries, Bible handbooks, and dictionaries. Set aside one or two hours weekly for study and interpretation, asking always for the Spirit to guide and speak to you clearly. Join a Bible study small group or cell group to study and share God's Word with others.

❦ Attend adult Bible class or Sunday school and Sunday services at your church so that you are regularly hearing God's Word. You may want to take a Bible or theology course at a nearby seminary or Bible college to help you into deeper study of God's Word.

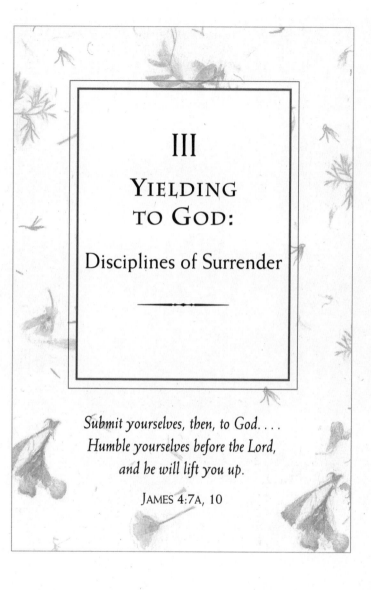

III

YIELDING TO GOD:

Disciplines of Surrender

———◆———

Submit yourselves, then, to God. . . .
Humble yourselves before the Lord,
and he will lift you up.

JAMES 4:7A, 10

7

Repentance and Confession

Charles Finney, America's greatest evangelist, through whom God sparked the second Great Awakening, was a man of pride and independence. While apprenticing in a law firm in Jefferson County, New York, Finney was slowly drawn near to God through the wooing of the Holy Spirit. His pride kept him from letting anyone know about his growing interest in God—he would cover the Bible he was reading with papers if someone came into the law office, or he would stuff the keyhole of his office door with a handkerchief in case anyone should try to peek through and observe him in prayer.

The day came, however, when Finney determined to accept Christ's offer of salvation. He crept deep into the woods until he found a secluded spot. He tried to pray but found his heart was not going out to God. Suddenly, he thought he heard someone approach, and he fearfully opened his eyes to see who was there. At that moment his pride—his concern for what others thought, his desire to be in control—was revealed to him by the Spirit to be the great difficulty that stood in the way.

Finney came under great conviction and godly sorrow for his wickedness in being ashamed to have someone see him on his knees before God. He cried out at the top of his lungs that he would not leave there if all the men on earth and all the devils in hell should stand around to watch. "What a sinner I am," he wept, "... ashamed to have any human being find me on my knees endeavoring to make my peace with my offended God."[1]

In that broken state, the Spirit brought a passage of Scripture to Finney's mind: "You will seek me and find me when you seek me with all your heart. I will be found by you" (Jer. 29:13–14). He seized on this promise like a drowning man reaching out for a life preserver. Aware of the present reality of God and convicted of his sin and brokenness, he was ready to surrender. Then and there, he gave his whole heart to God, receiving God's forgiveness and peace. Later that day, Finney was powerfully filled with the Spirit; within a few days, he was praying aloud in public for the first time in his life and preaching with such passion and force that many were brought to similar godly sorrow for sin and repentance. Revival was under way.[2]

Repentance and confession are the white flags of surrender we wave to declare the death of our pride and the submission of our will to God's will. Awareness and conviction of sin is the beginning of real Spirit-centered living. The disciplines of repentance and confession keep us on track in our journey toward true spirituality. They are at the heart of an open, growing relationship with God—outward signs of our inward desire to know and love God more fully. Repentance, says Oswald Chambers, "is the bedrock of Christianity."[3]

The Hebrew word for repent means "to turn away" or "to return," while the Greek word carries a sense of changing one's mind or purpose. So repentance is turning away from what we are thinking or doing, renouncing behaviors harmful to ourselves or others, surrendering those courses of action contrary to God's will and purpose, and returning to a loving and obedient relationship to him. True repentance brings revolution to the spiritual life, leading to the changing of our habits of thought, attitudes, outlook, and behavior. It is a "stretching exercise" of the spirit that helps us to get our lives out of the wrong shape and into the right shape of healthy surrender to God.

Sin, when cherished, becomes an obstacle to fellowship with God. If we want the Holy Spirit's transformation, we will be eager to eradicate sin from our lives by recognizing and renouncing it through confession and repentance. We will be like the psalmist, continually asking, "Search me, O God, and know my heart; test me and know my anxious thoughts. See if there is any offensive way in me, and lead me in the way everlasting" (Ps. 139:23–24).

Repentance and confession are disciplines of the Holy Spirit given to us by God to return us continually to a loving relationship with him. God desires to forgive his children, and we need to confess our sin so we might experience that forgiveness. Repentance and confession are not fearful responses to an angry master out to get us if we don't shape up. Rather, they are acts of anticipation and expectation. They are our response to the unconditional call of God's love.

Being a Christian necessarily involves us in the practice of regular lifelong repentance, which is the fruit of faith that springs from a human heart being renewed in God's heart. Through a lifetime of repentance and confession, we are helped by the Spirit to crucify "the sinful nature with its passions and desires," so that we can "live by the Spirit" and "keep in step with the Spirit" (Gal. 5:24–25).

The Work of the Spirit in Repentance and Confession

During his earthly ministry, Jesus promised he would send the Holy Spirit to us, and that "when he comes, he will convict the world of guilt in regard to sin and righteousness and judgment" (John 16:8). When the ache, anguish, and grief of repentance come crashing into our vain attempts at respectability and goodness, we can be sure that the Holy Spirit is at work forming the life of the Son of God in us. When we take time to reflect on our condition and to be aware of our sin, the Holy Spirit undertakes a deep, convicting, cleansing work within our hearts to lead us into repentance and confession.

True repentance is a gift of God, a result of godly sorrow that brings conviction that we have hurt and grieved God because of our sin (2 Cor. 7:10). "Against you, you only, have I sinned," says the psalmist (Ps. 51:4). True repentance always brings us to the point of saying, "I have sinned." With repentance, the focus is on God and not on our self-centered need to justify ourselves. The apostle Peter betrayed Jesus by denying he was one of Jesus' followers. Like Judas, Peter fell into sorrow and despair, but unlike Judas, Peter's sin brought him to a godly sorrow that worked toward repentance.[4]

"Repent and believe," are part of the first words we hear from Jesus in Mark's gospel (1:15). Jesus takes repentance seriously! Notice that whenever there is the slightest sign of repentance in the Gospels, Jesus is all over it. He knows that when repentance is happening, the Kingdom is advancing and people are coming to know the forgiving and forgetting nature of his Father. "There will be more rejoicing in heaven over one sinner who repents," Jesus says, "than over ninety-nine righteous persons who do not need to repent" (Luke 15:7). "Unless you repent," he warns, "you too will all perish" (Luke 13:3).

Blasphemy against the Holy Spirit is the one sin that cannot be forgiven (Matt. 12:22–37). Jesus tells this to some of the Pharisees who were slandering the Holy Spirit by giving the devil, and not the Holy Spirit, credit for Jesus' ability to cast out demons. The Pharisees' underlying sin was that they rejected the Spirit's work in bringing conviction regarding sin and truth. In doing so, they put themselves outside the bounds of God's mercy.

The Holy Spirit is the only force that can break our hard hearts and lead us to the repentance that is crucial for salvation and for sanctification. As we enter into the spiritual disciplines of repentance and confession, the Spirit enables us to "put to death the misdeeds of the body" (Rom. 8:13). The result is not sinless perfection, but an increasing ability, by the power of the Holy Spirit, to sin less and less as we grow into the heart of God. It is the Holy Spirit who helps us deal with sin and ultimately overcome it. We surrender to God through repentance and confession, thankful for the Holy Spirit's work in transforming us into the likeness of Jesus.

Steps in Repentance

Repentance begins with an awareness of sin and offense against God, which leads to sorrow and confession and brings a resolve to not sin again and to make restitution for wrongdoing.

Awareness of Sin and Offense Against God

Conviction of sin starts with an awareness that we have disobeyed God and, though we know what is right, we have said or done what is wrong. This first step in repentance is perhaps the most difficult because we are so prone to rationalizing our behavior, hiding our sinful actions from others, and becoming comfortable with self-deception (see James 1:22, 26). King David committed adultery with Bathsheba, had her husband Uriah murdered, lied about the whole affair, and went on as though nothing had happened, evidently thinking these events were of no concern to God and of no consequence to his spiritual life.

It was not until the prophet Nathan said to David, "You are the man," that David became aware of his sin and offense against God (2 Sam. 12:7). "For I know my transgressions," David cries out, "and my sin is always before me" (Ps. 51:3). The Holy Spirit shows up in our lives the way Nathan showed up in David's—convicting us of "guilt in regard to sin and righteousness and judgment" (John 16:8). True repentance comes only as we pass out of self-deception into awareness and conviction of sin.[5]

Sorrow and Remorse at Having Dishonored God

When confronted by Nathan, King David was so convicted of his sin that he was reduced to a state of complete sorrow and repentance. "Against you, you only, have I sinned and done what is evil in your sight" (Ps. 51:4). All sin is sin against God. We are not sinners because we engage in sin; we sin because we are sinners, rebellious and sinful from birth. David knows the inward rebellion and perversity of his human heart: "Surely I was sinful at birth, sinful from the time my mother conceived me" (Ps. 51:5). David appeals to God for mercy. He remembers God's "unfailing love" and "great compassion." He knows God will look favorably on a broken and contrite heart (Ps. 51:1, 17).

We know little about ourselves until we realize that we are sinful, that we dishonor God by our sin, that we cannot help ourselves, and that we need the transforming power of the Holy Spirit. In John's first letter, we read, "If we claim to be without sin, we deceive ourselves and the truth is not in us. If we confess our sins, he is faithful and just and will forgive us our sins and purify us from all unrighteousness. If we claim we have not sinned, we make him out to be a liar and his word has no place in our lives" (1 John 1:8–10).

Confession of Sin; Asking for Cleansing and Forgiveness

Godly sorrow leads naturally to confession, desire for forgiveness, and cleansing of conscience. David's prayer of repentance continues:

> Cleanse me with hyssop, and I will be clean; wash me, and I will be whiter than snow. Let me hear joy and gladness; let the bones you have crushed rejoice. Hide your face from my sins and blot out all my iniquity. Create in me a pure heart, O God, and renew a steadfast spirit within me. Do not cast me from your presence or take your Holy Spirit from me. Restore to me the joy of your salvation. (Ps. 51:7–12)

David has been crushed by his sin, rendered unable to move forward owing to the weight of sorrow and guilt upon him. He asks that his "bones"—his whole personality, spirit, and emotions—be made to rejoice, literally "to dance," from the assurance that mercy will be extended. David's words show the response of his human spirit to his good God, a response called forth and held in place by the presence and power of the Holy Spirit.[6]

When Doug's best friend in elementary school, Bruce, ran for president of their sixth grade class, Doug was his campaign manager. Doug outdid himself making posters and encouraging classmates to vote for Bruce, but on election day—at the last minute and pretending lofty motives—Doug voted for Bruce's opponent. In his heart he was jealous, unable to take joy in his best friend's potential success.

Bruce lost the election by one vote. Doug was overcome by sorrow and remorse. By the grace of God, though he could not have explained it at the time, he received a broken and contrite spirit. He knew in his heart that he was not worthy of Bruce's friendship. When Bruce asked Doug how he voted, Doug was able to be honest and tell Bruce what he had done and that he was sorry. He begged Bruce to forgive him, and he did. The two went on being best friends, even when Doug was elected class president the next semester.

Henri Nouwen writes: "Confession and forgiveness are the concrete forms in which we sinful people love one another."[7] When risks are taken, confession given, and forgiveness spoken, a real encounter takes place in which the reconciling and healing power of the Holy Spirit can be experienced. Through confession, what is kept in darkness and has festered in secret is brought into the light and made visible, losing its power to shame and weaken us. Through forgiveness, the darkness is dispelled and healing flows both to the individual and within the community.

Resolving Not to Engage in the Sin Again

If we are truly repentant, the Holy Spirit will create in us a pure heart that hates sin and is set on overcoming it, and a renewed, steadfast, and willing spirit bent on resisting temptation to sin. Part of this process is to know our particular areas of weakness. In doing so, we can learn to avoid situations where temptation is strong and ask others to hold us accountable in those areas.

For Siang-Yang, he knows that his extended family carries a history of having short tempers. He takes pride in the fact that, according to his brother-in-law, he has the best self-control and easiest disposition among his brothers and sisters. However, on occasion, he has used his family history as an excuse to justify whatever anger he does have. Recently, the Holy Spirit has been convicting him that when he is tired or running late, or when he is quick-tempered with his wife or children, his behavior is not pleasing to God. Siang-Yang now views his temper as an area of repentance. He acknowledges his need for God's mercy and transforming power in renewing his spirit and enabling him to resist the temptation to be angry.

Paul recognized that godly sorrow had a powerful effect on the Corinthian church. "See what this godly sorrow has produced in you: what earnestness, what eagerness to clear yourselves, what indignation, what alarm, what longing, what concern, what readiness to see justice done," he says in 2 Corinthians 7:11. The Corinthians proved their repentance by doing everything they could to change the situation their sinful actions had produced. They had come to see the wrongness of their behavior and pledged to Paul and Titus and one another by their actions that they would never do it again.[8]

Seeking Restitution and Reconciliation

Part of what it means to act on the resolve not to sin again is to set things as right as we can within our ability and power. Zacchaeus committed himself to make a fourfold restitution to those hurt by the excesses of his tax collecting. Worldly sorrow for sin resents that the sin has been found out; godly sorrow for sin, seeing the fundamental evil involved, sets about restoring what's been lost and mending what's been broken.

Jesus encourages us to seek reconciliation when we have sinned against another: "If you are offering your gift at the altar and there remember that your brother has something against you, leave your gift there in front of the altar. First go and be reconciled to your brother; then come and offer your gift" (Matt. 5:23–24). When someone has sinned against us, we are to go to them, lay out the issue, and seek understanding and reconciliation (Matt. 18:15–17). Sin separates us from God and others. Our restitution and heartfelt seeking after reconciliation is a concrete sign of our surrender to God and desire to be in right fellowship with him and others.

Confession and Self-examination

Humans are experts in the art of self-deception—"If we say we have no sin, we deceive ourselves, and the truth is not in us" (1 John 1:8 RSV). But through regular self-examination, we can become aware of our true condition. "Examine yourselves," Paul admonished, "to see whether you are in the faith; test yourselves" (2 Cor. 13:5). Self-examination that leads to confession helps us to discern who we are before God and in relation to others.

Brother Lawrence provides a wonderful model of a life lived by self-examination and confession in the presence of God. Lawrence was in constant conversation with God as he engaged in the most simple and mundane tasks of living. When he finished any task or duty, he examined how he had discharged his duty; if he found he had done well, he returned thanks to God; if otherwise, he asked pardon, and without being discouraged, he set his mind right again and continued his exercise of the presence of God as if he had never deviated from it. "Thus," he said, "by rising after my falls, and by frequently renewed acts of faith and love, I am come to a state wherein it would be as difficult for me not to think of God as it was at first to accustom myself to it."[9]

Self-examination is at the heart of a growing, vibrant relationship with God. It is growth-producing to take time each day or each week to review what has been happening. To ask, "Have I been responsive to God's leading today? Did I speak the truth in love? Did I give in to the temptation to pass on idle gossip? Was I angry, lustful, jealous, fearful, envious? Have I been only with those who can reward me for my service or have I also done it 'for one of the least of these?' (Matt. 25:45). Is my mind set on the things of the Spirit or am I gratifying the desires of the flesh? (see Gal. 5:16–24)." One way to go about this would be to review what Jesus says comes out of our hearts and pollutes us—"evil thoughts, sexual immorality, theft, murder, adultery, greed, malice, deceit, lewdness, envy, slander, arrogance and folly" (Mark 7:20–22). It is a rewarding challenge to regularly examine ourselves to see if we are holding to our faith.

Corporate Confession

We are commanded in Scripture to "confess your sins to each other and pray for each other" (James 5:16). This experience can be so positive and strengthening it should be worked into the fabric of every Christian life. When you confess your sins to someone you trust and who knows you well, several things happen. As your sin is exposed to the light, it loses much of its power to control you. It is no longer the dark, looming force that easily crushes you with shame and guilt. In the light, sin is exposed for what it is: a wrong behavior or attitude which can be forgiven, healed, and transformed. Light overcomes darkness. The very act of telling someone what we have done, or failed to do, is the beginning of returning to God, of turning around and walking in the opposite direction.

When we confess our sins to a trusted friend, counselor, or spiritual director, we commit ourselves to efforts to not lapse that way again. We can find great support and power through friendships and prayer groups where we, by choice, are held accountable for spiritual practices—regular Scripture study, self-examination, prayer, and service to others—and pledge to give honest answers to questions regarding temptations we have faced, sins committed, and the character of our personal walk with God.

Corporate confession creates a context in which we can hear a pronouncement of forgiveness, bringing us into an experience of the reality that God forgives us. "If we confess our sins, he is faithful and just and will forgive us our sins and purify us from all unrighteousness" (1 John 1:9). Brothers and sisters who act as confessors in our lives help us to be transparent and vulnerable with God. In reacting to us as God does, without condemnation or reproach, but with grace, wisdom, and counsel, these confessors proclaim the mercy and forgiveness of God.

A colleague at Fuller Seminary, angry one day, carried her frustration into a lunch meeting with a good friend. As she became aware of the degree to which her anger was blocking being present with her friend, she said, "Would you be my confessor?" The friend agreed, and she laid out her frustration, let go of hurt feelings, forgave the person who had hurt her, and asked God's forgiveness for holding on to bitterness instead of trusting God to be at work. The friend prayed forgiveness over her, declaring the authority and truth of Scripture from 1 John 1:9. Her anger dissipated and she was free to move on in conversation, giving attention to her friend.

A form of corporate confession referred to as "identificational repentance" involves identifying sin committed generationally and geographically, accepting responsibility for that sin and repenting of it, and asking God to forgive, cleanse, and restore the blessing that was lost as a result of the sin. Nehemiah, removed generationally and geographically from his people, nonetheless identified with the sins of his forbears, saying, "Hear the prayer your servant is praying before you day and night for your servants, the people of Israel. I confess the sins we Israelites, including myself and my father's house, have committed against you. We have acted very wickedly toward you" (Neh. 1:6–7).

In our day, identificational repentance is taking place as German Christians gather in the Netherlands to repent for the atrocities of the Nazi era, as New Zealand Christians confess sins against the native Maoris, as Anglo-American Christians say prayers of atonement and repentance in locations where native American peoples were massacred, and as various denominational groups in America are repenting and asking forgiveness from African-Americans for endorsing slavery. Pope John Paul II has "demanded that his church publicly repent for sins committed by Catholics across history in errant, overzealous defense of their faith."[10] God is calling the body of Christ to be Nehemiahs for our families, denominations, cities, and nations.

Confession Brings Healing and Forgiveness

We are commanded to confess to and pray for each other "so that you may be healed" (James 5:16). The power of the Holy Spirit is at work through confession to bring healing to our spirits, minds, emotions, and bodies. When we confess our sins we establish, or reestablish, Christ's authority and Lordship in that area of our lives. As we repent of any idolatry or other behavior that has weakened our attachment to Christ, we open the door for the Holy Spirit's healing power to flow forth.

Experts tell us that we are in self-deception, we too easily allow sin, brokenness, and rebellion—things that Jesus says come from within—to consume and drive us. We are often seemingly unaware that we are placing our trust in ourselves or in material things rather than in Christ. We are blinded by false idolatries that compromise our submission and obedience to Jesus.

In praying for others, people are often surprised when the Holy Spirit reveals to them that Jesus is not Lord in specific areas of their lives—that, for example, we have allowed fear or anger or lust to have more power and authority in specific situations than Jesus! As we confess, we reestablish God's authority in these areas, and healing begins to flow.

Hidden shame from past sin and abuse—even when we are innocent victims—holds us back from the healing and joy that the Lord promises. Through confession to another person of sin committed or abuse received, the power of shame is broken. Our own brokenness receives the light of God's grace and is healed.

It is the truth that makes us free. No sin is beyond God's forgiveness: "There is now no condemnation for those who are in Christ Jesus" (Rom. 8:1). In Christ, we are able to rebuke shame, fear, and anything else that compromises the lordship of Jesus. Through confession, we give Christ permission to overcome these things by his blood, and the Holy Spirit strengthens us to receive the fullness of God's grace and mercy. Our repentance and confession, our acknowledgment of Christ's lordship, opens the way to healing, growth, and maturity in him.

Confession as the Prelude to Renewal and Revival

If my people, who are called by my name, will humble themselves and pray and seek my face and turn from their wicked ways, then will I hear from heaven and will forgive their sin and will heal their land," promises 2 Chronicles 7:14. Throughout church history, there is a remarkable correlation between heartfelt repentance and confession on the part of God's people and mighty visitations of the Holy Spirit that bring conviction of sin to the wider community. Getting right with God opens the floodgates of God's mercy and releases the power of the Spirit for revival.

In the months before the powerful outbreak of revival in the Hebrides Islands in 1949, several men in the village of Sharda were prompted by the Spirit to pray together three nights a week for a spiritual awakening. Duncan Campbell described what happened:

> For months they waited upon God in this manner. Nothing happened, until one night ... one young man, taking his Bible in his hand, read from Psalm 24, 'Who shall ascend the hill of God and who shall stand in his holy presence? He that hath clean hands and a pure heart, who hath not lifted up his soul unto vanity nor sworn deceitfully; he shall receive the blessing of the Lord.' He shut his Bible and, looking down at his companions, said this, 'Brethren, it seems to me just so much humbug waiting as we are waiting, praying as we are praying, unless we ourselves are rightly related to God.' He then began to pray, and in his prayer he asked God to reveal to him if his hands were clean, if his heart was pure.... At that moment, something happened in that barn. A power was let loose that shook the parish from center to circumference.... God had visited them and neither they nor the parish could ever be the same again.[11]

One of the very best things we can do for growth in Christ is to cultivate for ourselves a willing spirit of repentance. J. I. Packer states, "As the single-mindedness of our inward devotion is the real index of the quality of our discipleship, so the thoroughness of our daily repentance is the real index of the quality of our devotion."[12] Repentance and confession are the first steps into surrender. Through these disciplines, we begin to walk in humility away from the root of inward corruption centered in pride. Repentance and confession are antidotes to our pride—they kill it! But we are getting ahead of ourselves. The breaking of our pride in yielding and surrendering to God and his purposes is the focus of our next chapter.

Entering In

The things God wants to do in and through us cannot happen unless our hearts are broken and contrite. Until we are filled with a "godly sorrow that leads to repentance," unless we are done trying to stand up and defend ourselves, our hope is still in ourselves and not in God alone. The Holy Spirit convicts us of sin and draws us into repentance, causing us to cry out with King David for a clean heart and a right spirit. The Holy Spirit can rebuild the broken walls that have resulted from our rebellion and sin. May his love and power be manifest in our midst in fresh, dynamic, life-giving ways.

Right now:

Ask the Lord to search your heart, as David did: "Search me, O God, and know my heart; test me and know my anxious thoughts. See if there is any offensive way in me, and lead me in the way everlasting" (Ps. 139:23–24). Ask the Holy Spirit to shed light into the deepest area of your heart and bring knowledge and conviction of any sin. Lay before the Lord what the Spirit reveals. Ask him to help you, beginning today, to cultivate a willing spirit of repentance.

In the coming days and weeks:

❧ Each day this week, talk to God and listen to him regarding any unhealthy areas of pride in your life. Ask the Lord, "Does my pride, concern for what others think, and desire to control stand in the way of closer relation to you, as it did for Charles Finney?" If you are human, the answer is probably yes. Let the Spirit identify at least one area of pride or control to submit to him. Repent and ask for strength and resolve to act in new ways. Remember that conviction of sin starts with awareness of sin.

❧ Each day for a week or two, pray Psalm 51. Review the steps in repentance: awareness, remorse, confession, resolve, restitution. Take time for the Holy Spirit to clarify your situation and give you a godly sorrow for sin.

❧ Take time this week to let the Holy Spirit show you whom to love. Is there anyone you have wronged, cheated, dismissed, or hurt (i.e., a colleague at work, a classmate, a parent, or child)? Ask, "How can I make this right? What restitution should I undertake? Will you help me, Holy Spirit, to love and serve this person today?" If someone has wronged you, set your will on forgiving them and trust the Spirit to provide opportunity for that forgiveness to work its way through to reconciliation.

❧ Explore a more regular practice of self-examination. Think about the following questions (with your small group or accountability partner, if possible) asked regularly in the small group Methodist meetings of John Wesley's day:
What known sins have you committed since our last meeting?
What temptations have you struggled with?
How were you delivered from temptations?
What have you thought, said, or done which you have questioned whether or not it was sin?
Have you anything you desire to keep secret?

❧ Are you burdened by any sin or secret shame you haven't been able to confess to anyone before? Lay your burden down with a counselor or spiritual advisor. By allowing the sin or shame to be exposed to the light, it will lose its power to control and create fear. Receive forgiveness and acceptance from God through your confessor and return to the Father's loving embrace. Read Luke 15:11–24 to be reminded of God's overwhelming love in welcoming back the broken and lost. Receive and celebrate God's loving forgiveness toward you and rejoice that "there is now no condemnation for those who are in Christ Jesus" (Rom. 8:1).

8

Yielding and Submission

———•◆•———

I pray for you, Paul wrote to the Ephesians, that God, "out of his glorious riches ... may strengthen you with power through his Spirit in your inner being, so that Christ may dwell in your hearts through faith ... that you, being rooted and established in love, may have power, together with all the saints, to grasp how wide and long and high and deep is the love of Christ, and to know this love that surpasses knowledge—that you may be filled to the measure of all the fullness of God" (Eph. 3:16–19).

Do you want the fullness of God? Do you really desire more of the love of God? Do you yearn for love, the fruit of the Spirit, to be manifested through you? If so, the way in is through yielding and submission. While repentance and confession are the first steps in surrender, regular and habitual yielding and submission are the sure and steady strides of surrender into the fullness of the heart of God. We must stand with John the Baptist, who said, "He must become greater; I must become less" (John 3:30).

As we enter the disciplines of yielding and submission, as we "become less" and our wills are submitted more and more to his will, we can expect a tidal wave of God's love to carry us straight into all the fullness of God. Yielding to God involves the most passionate love and desire; it is the natural fruit of a growing love affair with the divine. As we surrender, we become, by the power of the Spirit, so much one with our Lord that the thought of what we have given up never enters our minds. Oswald Chambers said, " ... take an absolute plunge into the love of God, and when you are there you will be amazed at your foolishness for not getting there before."[1]

To surrender means giving oneself over to the possession or power of another; to give up, relinquish, submit, or yield. With all our fleshly desires, it's no wonder we cringe when we hear these words. We naturally want to maintain control and secure our own futures. We don't want to be beholden or obligated to anyone. But while this seems the natural way of life to us, in actuality it is the way of death. We must lose our "natural" selves to find our true selves. Jesus said, "Unless a kernel of wheat falls to the ground and dies, it remains only a single seed. But if it dies, it produces many seeds. The man who loves his life will lose it, while the man who hates his life in this world will keep it for eternal life" (John 12:24–25).

Surrendering means the husk of our individual independence from God is broken and our personality is liberated to be yielded in dependence on him, to be one with his will and purpose. The Holy Spirit cannot work fully unless we are yielded to him. A fundamental battle for control is under way. Will it be our way or his way? Will we give up all things for the sake of the only thing worth having: life with God himself? God wants our surrender. Christ says, "Hand over the whole natural self, all the desires which you think innocent as well as the ones you think wicked— the whole outfit. I will give you a new self instead. In fact, I will give you Myself: my own will shall become yours."[2]

Receiving a new self is enough reason to hand over the whole natural self. But there are a few more reasons why God requires yielding and submission before he fills, changes, and blesses us.

First, surrender to God is good for us. It is what we are made for. St. Augustine said, "Our hearts are restless until they find their rest in Thee." God knows that surrender to him brings us the greatest contentment and happiness. As François Fénelon wrote:

> What God asks of us is a will which is no longer divided between him and any creature. It is a will pliant in his hand which neither seeks nor rejects anything, which wants without reserve whatever he wants, and which never wants under

any pretext anything which he does not want. When we are in this disposition, all is well, and the most idle amusements turn to good works. Happy are those who give themselves to God.[3]

Paul understood the larger purpose of human transformation that God has for us through yielding and submission. "I have been crucified with Christ," he rejoices, "and I no longer live, but Christ lives in me. The life I live in the body, I live by faith in the Son of God, who loved me and gave himself for me" (Gal. 2:20). The secret of being content in every situation, says Paul, remains in, and comes from remaining in, the one who gives him strength (Phil. 4:12–13). Union with and surrender to the living, exalted Christ is the secret of contentment and the source of Paul's abiding strength (see 2 Cor. 12:9–10). Much of what God has for us we cannot receive unltil we surrender.

Second, yielding to God brings freedom from introspection and the sins of the self-life—self-praise, self-sufficiency, self-loathing, self-absorption, self-abuse, self-indulgence, and others like them. Yielding brings freedom from the burden of having to control everything and having everything our own way. It means freedom to listen to others, to care for their needs, and to serve them in love.

Finally, submission to God cultivates the mind of Christ in us. As we connect with the Spirit through yielding and submission, we are more open to God, more sensitive to God's presence, more discerning of God's will, more humble in the pattern of Jesus. Submission is the concrete expression of our desire to enter into the fullness of God.

The Work of the Holy Spirit in Yielding and Submission

In our hearts we are to "set apart Christ as Lord" (1 Peter 3:15). It is impossible to surrender in this way without the work of the Holy Spirit. "No one," says Paul, "can say, 'Jesus is Lord,' except by the Holy Spirit" (1 Cor. 12:3). The Spirit of Truth guides us into all truth, convicting us especially of the truth about Jesus. The Spirit brings no glory to himself, but promotes the glory of Christ (John 16:13–14), declaring him to be our only rightful Lord. The beginning of our surrender is acknowledgement, by the power of the Holy Spirit, that Christ, full of grace and truth, in whom we see the glory of the Father (John 1:14), is our true Savior, Master, and King.

We are to live, says Paul, not according to our sinful nature, but according to the Spirit—with our "minds set on what the Spirit desires," having minds "controlled by the Spirit," which is "life and peace" (Rom. 8:5–6). Apart from the Spirit, we are in bondage to our sinful human nature—trapped in death, hostile to God, self-indulgent and disobedient, unacceptable to God (Rom. 8:6–8).

As we live according to the Holy Spirit, however, by yielding to the directing and empowering ministry of the Spirit, we walk in the victory of grace over law. Being led by God's Spirit becomes a primary mark of our relationship to Jesus. "The Spirit himself testifies with our spirit that we are God's children" (Rom. 8:14, 16). We are admonished not to go on living to the flesh, but to submit to life in the Spirit, thus causing death to all selfish actions and so gaining real life.

Our obligation then is to live according to the Spirit! We are to be led by the Spirit and to "keep in step with the Spirit" (Gal. 5:16, 25). We are also to bear the fruit of the Spirit—"love, joy, peace, patience, kindness, goodness, faithfulness, gentleness and self-control" (Gal. 5:22–23). These qualities are to be recognizable as being a result of the Spirit of God working directly on the human heart. This "fruit" that Paul speaks of is therefore not possible, or at least not natural, to one who has not surrendered to God. It is love, for example (and we could insert any fruit of the Spirit in place of "love") that caused Jesus to pray for those who murdered him. It is love, born in us by the Holy Spirit, that provides motivation for us to pray for our enemies. It is love that loves the unlovely, that forgives seventy times seven, that humbles itself in front of colleagues, that is patient and kind, that is not self-seeking or easily angered, that keeps no record of wrongs, and that rejoices with the truth (1 Cor. 13:4–6).

Here we are at the very heart of the work of the Spirit to transform us. The fruits of the Spirit are not qualities to practice or perform. We cannot make these things happen in us. They are the result of the Holy Spirit impregnating the life of Jesus in us, of our lives and character being steadily transformed into the beauty of Christ.

It is wrong, however, to think that because only the Holy Spirit can transform our lives, we are to sit back and assume there is nothing for us to do. We work and God works. The Scripture is full of admonishments for us to resist the devil, to stand fast, to fight the good fight, to touch nothing unclean, to put to death what is earthly in us, to put on love. If God's work is to be accomplished in us, we must be cooperating with him daily through the spiritual disciplines of regular prayer, study of Scripture, spiritual warfare, confession, and submission. Such prayer, study, and warfare must be *in the strength of the Spirit*, not in the energy of the flesh: "If by the Spirit you put to death the misdeeds of the body, you will live" (Rom. 8:13); "Be strong in the Lord and in his mighty power" (Eph. 6:10); "righteousness, peace and joy" come in the Holy Spirit (Rom. 14:17).

Paul's whole ministry to the Gentiles was to present the Word of God in its fullness—"Christ in you, the hope of glory" (Col. 1:27). "For this I toil," Paul said, "striving with all the energy which he mightily inspires within me" (Col. 1:29 RSV). God expects us to toil and strive with all the strength we have, but along the journey it is the Holy Spirit who changes us into his likeness, from one degree of glory to another (2 Cor. 3:18).[4]

Andrew Murray summarizes for us:

> The Spirit teaches me to yield my will entirely to the will of the Father. He opens my ear to wait in great gentleness and teachableness of soul for what the Father has day by day to speak and to teach. He discovers to me how union with God's will is union with God Himself; how entire surrender to God's will is the Father's claim, the Son's example, and the true blessedness of the soul.[5]

Our Model of Submission

Jesus habitually submitted his will to his Father, leaving control completely in his Father's hands. In contrast, we try to organize, control, and manage things with all the sanctified energy and creativity we can muster. We say we must do all we can for God. Jesus says we must let God do all he will. For Jesus, surrender was the most natural expression of his passion and loyalty to the Father: "The Son can do nothing by himself; he can only do what he sees his Father doing, because whatever the Father does the Son also does" (John 5:19). Jesus is the model of absolute submission to the Father's will. Surrender to God is the source of his freedom and the foundation of his earthly authority.

Paul, in his letter to the Philippians, gives us a wonderful passage describing the humility, weakness, and obedience of Jesus (Phil. 2:6–9). Jesus literally "emptied himself," putting aside his divine prerogatives, refusing to hang on to the glory he shared with his Father. In so doing, he reversed all notions of greatness and power. He became weak that we might become strong; he became poor that we might become rich (see 2 Cor. 8:9); he became a servant and died for us, that we might die to ourselves and become servants of others. We are to have his same attitude of self-sacrificing humility and love for others (Phil. 2:2–5).

We are called by Jesus to life-giving and life-receiving surrender: "If anyone would come after me, he must deny himself and take up his cross and follow me. For whoever wants to save his life will lose it, but whoever loses his life for me and for the gospel will save it" (Mark 8:34–35). Again, Jesus said to them, "The greatest among you will be your servant. For whoever exalts himself will be humbled, and whoever humbles himself will be exalted" (Matt. 23:11–12).

Before his death, Jesus shared a last meal with his disciples. They had come from the dusty road to a borrowed "upper room" for the meal, but there was no household servant present to wash their feet. It would not have occurred to any of the disciples to perform this most menial task for the others, but Jesus, in an unforgettable picture of submission, washed the disciples' feet. "Do you understand what I have done for you?" he asked them. "You call me 'Teacher' and 'Lord,' and rightly so, for that is what I am. Now that I, your Lord and Teacher, have washed your feet, you also should wash one another's feet. I have set you an example that you should do as I have done for you" (John 13:12–15).

Jesus demonstrates for us the nature of true authority. He had legitimate power to change lives, but he exercised this power to serve others. People saw the very clear healing, helping, saving purpose in his exercise of authority. "He used power over them to heal, never to demand. He cured their diseases and asked nothing from them. He claimed to be Lord, yet used his lordship to liberate them. He claimed to be Master, yet he nurtured people into freedom," says noted author Lewis Smedes.[6] In complete submission to his Father's will, he won trust and gained authority in the lives of others by serving them without enslaving them. This is the mind we are to have among ourselves.

"What we have to realize," says J. I. Packer, "is that we grow *up* into Christ by growing *down* into lowliness (humility, from the Latin word *humilis*, meaning low). Christians, we might say, grow greater by getting smaller."[7] Growth in the spiritual life is advance into personal insignificance that allows the majesty of Christ's grace to shine through us. When we come under conviction of sin and our pride is broken, we begin to surrender our fantasies of omnicompetence and see ourselves more realistically—as less attractive, less able, less perceptive, less dependable, less devoted than we like to think and want others to think we are.

When we stop having to be indispensable and admired for doing everything well, we can surrender to the truth that we are dispensable and insignificant in the total scheme of things. When we realize that we can do nothing that is of lasting significance apart from Jesus (John 15:5), we are ready to have the Spirit prove through us that we can do everything in him who gives us strength (Phil. 4:13). Not my will, but "thy will be done." The truly surrendered Christian is content to curl up small, as it were, to be "transformed into [Jesus'] likeness with ever-increasing glory" by the power of the Holy Spirit (2 Cor. 3:18).

In the twelfth century, St. Francis of Assisi, curling up small and becoming like Jesus, exerted a powerful attraction on the people of his day. To read the *Little Flowers of St. Francis*[8] is to discover a man surrendered to God in love, lost in the joy of relationship to Christ. Francis's life, like that of Jesus his Lord, reveals so much to us about what is happening in the heart of God: not cold power, but self-sacrificing humility; not unquestioned authority, but patient, enduring love and forgiveness; not detached judgment, but relentless welcoming and giving. There seems to be no bottom to Francis's grateful heart. Eyewitnesses testified that Francis was so filled with gladness he would pick up a stick, place it across his arm like a bow on a violin, and play, dance, and sing to the Lord in an ecstasy of joy.

Following Jesus means yielding our wills moment by moment to the control of the Holy Spirit and staying fully surrendered to Christ the Son and God the Father. Each new day we should consider ourselves dead to our old sinful tendencies and alive to God in Christ Jesus (Rom. 6:4–11). Paul wrote to the Corinthians that they should no longer live for themselves, but only for him who died and rose again on their behalf (2 Cor. 5:15).

Thomas Kelly, a twentieth-century Quaker, writes: "The life that intends to be wholly obedient, wholly submissive, wholly listening, is astonishing in its completeness. Its joys are ravishing, its peace profound, its humility the deepest, its power world shaking, its love enveloping, its simplicity that of a trusting child."[9]

Areas of Yielding

The moment-by-moment surrender of our wills to the control of the Holy Spirit involves yielding to God, to Scripture, and to one another.

Yielding to God

"Submit yourselves, then, to God.... Humble yourselves before the Lord, and he will lift you up" (James 4:7, 10). There is only one being deserving of our absolute submission, and that is the God we have come to know in Jesus Christ. As long as we are yielding to the Lord Jesus Christ, we can be sure that we are safeguarded in all our acts of submission. Of course, the purpose of *all* the spiritual disciplines is that we may say yes to God in *all* our life, every day. However, the discipline of yielding is most direct in bringing our bodies, minds, and spirits into daily surrender to God. As we pray to be guided by the Holy Spirit in expressing the mind of Christ in all our circumstances, we experience new freedom. As we begin to walk in the freedom of daily surrender to Christ, our character is changed.

Several years ago Doug was invited back to his college alma mater to preach at a Sunday chapel service. He was highly honored by the invitation and spent a few weeks in self-congratulation (not failing to mention the invitation to every possible person) and generally esteeming himself more highly than he ought. He was certainly not growing up into Christ by growing down into lowliness!

At the end of the Sunday chapel, after what Doug thought was a memorable preaching effort, he was handed a two-hundred-dollar honorarium. That was a huge amount at the time, the biggest honorarium by far Doug had ever received for a preaching assignment. He was thrilled!

On the way home on the plane, he daydreamed about all the ways he could spend the two hundred dollars. In the midst of his reverie, the Holy Spirit intervened. Doug believes he heard the Lord say very distinctly in his spirit, "I want you to give that money away." "What?" Doug exclaimed. "I deserve that money. I earned it. It's mine to do with as I please!" The Lord responded, "Everything you have is from me. I gave you the talent and ability and opportunity that led to that invitation; I have the right to tell you how to use that money. It will be good for you to give it away, trust me. Besides, you've been asking me to give you my mind about things, and so I am. I want you to give that money away."

Doug struggled with this exchange all the way home, but by the time he got off the plane, he was determined to yield to the Spirit's leading. A few days later he surrendered, giving the money away anonymously (at the prompting of the Spirit, who was working to curb his pride). As the money left his hands, he felt one last pang, and then an immense exhilaration at being free from the need to have control over it. It was a great learning and changing time for him, and ever since then Doug permits the Holy Spirit to tell him how to use any money he receives.

Through habitual surrender to God, we live closer to the truth about ourselves, others, and the world around us. We grow in humility, becoming fertile ground (from the Latin "humus," the root word for humility) for the transforming work of the Holy Spirit.

Yielding to Scripture

If our only act of complete surrender is to the person of God, we yield to him most effectively through submission to his Word (see chapter 6). We depend upon the Holy Spirit to interpret the Word of God for us and to give us the insight to apply it to our situations. In obedience, again by the power of the Spirit, we act upon the Word in our daily lives and relationships.

Early in his new life of commitment to Christ, St. Francis was eager to receive vocational clarity from God. After mass one day, he prayed with Brother Bernard that Christ would reveal to them through the Scripture his path of obedience for them. Opening the Bible, their eyes fell on the words, "If you wish to be perfect, go, sell all that you have, and give to the poor, and come, follow Me." A second time they opened the Scripture and read, "Take nothing for your journey, neither staff, nor wallet, nor bread, nor money." And yet a third time they opened and read, "If anyone wishes to come after Me, let him deny himself, and take up his cross, and follow Me." Closing the Bible, Francis exclaimed to Bernard that this was the counsel of Christ and that they should go and do perfectly what Christ commanded them.[10]

The renewal movement that Francis founded in obedience to these simple commands of Jesus shook the entire world of his day. We too will be in for renewal and shaking when we yield to the

Scripture and ask the Holy Spirit to speak to us through the Word and apply its truths to our lives.

Yielding to One Another

"Be subject to one another out of reverence for Christ," writes Paul (Eph. 5:21 NRSV), and "in humility consider others better than yourselves. Each of you should look not only to your own interests, but also to the interests of others" (Phil. 2:3–4).

Here is where we run into some difficulty. Submission to other human beings can become destructive, and when it does, it is contrary to the mind of Christ. Both Peter and Paul counsel that it is sometimes necessary to resist human authority out of obedience to Christ. The key to healthy submission is to choose, out of our freedom and identity in Christ, to have his mind about things.

We have already examined Jesus as our model of submission. He won authority with others by serving them without enslaving them. We are to serve others in this same way, and to give our willing submission to those who seek to lead us as servants. Having the mind of Christ, with his love as the plumb line, keeps submission from becoming distorted or destructive.

Love is the fundamental standard for Paul in his call for mutual submission between husbands and wives (Eph. 5). Wives are to be subject to their husbands not because of cultural expectation or natural order but because submission is the style for *all* Christians, including husbands. The Christian gospel launched a revolution of mutual respect, affirmation, and service. There are no "high" or "low" positions in Christian marriage, nor in the entire Christian family. A new order has begun in which all participants regard themselves as servants of one Master and submit themselves in mutual service to one another "out of reverence for Christ."

The revolution of mutual submission can occur whenever we are in relation with others—in the family, with neighbors, at the workplace, in church settings, and with those we meet in the course of daily life. We submit to others by being patient, compassionate, willing to go the extra mile, and encouraging. Small acts of kindness that require limited time and energy—such as writing a note, helping with a task, or visiting a sick friend—begin to build habits of humility and train the heart for the more demanding work of submission.

Small acts of kindness were the "little way" of St. Therese of Lisieux, who willingly accepted the most menial tasks and gladly accepted unjust criticism as a means of serving Christ. By seeking out those nuns in her order who were thought to be particularly unpleasant and finding ways to love and serve them, she trusted the Spirit to form in her the humble heart of Jesus.[11]

Are you surrounded by people you don't respect or who don't respect you? Love them the way Christ loves you! Have you allowed any to become your enemies at church or work? Pray for them today and find hidden ways to serve them. Identify with God's interest in people. Look at others through the eyes of Jesus. What does he see? How is he praying? How can you cooperate with him in his eternal work?

The knowledge that God has loved us to the utmost, to the end of all our sin and selfishness, giving his own life for each one of us, should send us into life to love in the same way. While we cannot "perform" this out of our flesh, we can out of our surrender to him, as his love is shed abroad in our hearts by the Holy Spirit. Oswald Chambers said:

> When I am possessed by God it is not that He gives me power to love like He does, but that the very nature of God loves through me. Just as he put up with the things in me which were not of Him, so He puts up with the things which are not of Him in others through me, and what is manifested is the love of God, the love that suffers long and is kind, the love that does not take account of evil, the love that never fails.[12]

Jesus commanded love—"love one another"—and defined it—"as I have loved you." It's not sentimental Hollywood; it's not words without deeds; and it's not optional. It is what Christ did and what we are called to do: "By this everyone will know that you are my disciples" (John 13:34–35 NRSV). We are to be identified by our love! Not "if you have the right doctrine," not "if you get the best grades," not "if you say the politically correct thing," not "if you are diligent, loyal, and successful in your work." The only Christ-certified mark of discipleship is our love for one another. Are you recognized by others for your love?

Full Surrender

As we enter the spiritual disciplines of yielding and submission, we can expect a tidal wave of God's love to carry us straight into all the fullness of God. As we surrender, we become, by the power of the Holy Spirit, so much one with our Lord that the thought of what we are losing never enters our minds. We are made for complete surrender to God. It is the one thing which will allow him the freedom necessary to transform our lives and use us effectively in ministry.

Until he has our whole hearts, we are like pieces of clay that keep moving around on the potter's wheel, unwilling to stay put long enough to be shaped and molded by the potter. Needless to say, this situation makes for some really funny-looking pots. When we are willing to fully surrender, to remain in place (John 15:4–5), allowing the potter to do with us what he chooses, he will transform us into vessels suitable for his use. Andrew Murray said, "Every one of us is a temple of God in which God will dwell and work mightily on one condition—absolute surrender to Him. God claims it, God is worthy of it, and without it God cannot work His blessed work in us."[13]

Our readiness to surrender is itself a sign that the Spirit has been powerfully at work in drawing us near to God in intimate relationship, convicting us of sin and brokenness, and building our trust and confidence in the love and faithfulness of the one to whom we surrender. Surrender, then, becomes the sweetest, most perceptive, and wisest thing we can do. Our motivation for surrender is relationship with the One in whom we receive the fullness of love, joy, peace, hope, and contentment.

Entering In

As we prepare to enter in, we can sing and pray with confident assurance the old hymn "I Surrender All."

> All to Jesus I surrender,
> Make me Savior, wholly Thine.
> Let me feel the Holy Spirit,
> Truly know that Thou art mine.
> All to Jesus I surrender,
> Lord, I give myself to Thee;
> Fill me with Thy love and power,
> Let Thy blessing fall on me.[14]

Right now:

Pray:

Lord, I want to know the love that surpasses knowledge and to be filled to the measure of all the fullness of God. I yield to you now, as much as I am able, and ask you, Holy Spirit, to lead me deeper into surrender. I want to be identified by my love for you and for others. Lead me in the days and weeks to come into this great, risky, vulnerable adventure of loving as you have loved. Thank you for your promise to be with me to the end. In Jesus' name, Amen.

In the coming days and weeks:

❧ Pray meditatively through chapter 2 of Paul's letter to the Philippians. What does Jesus' model of voluntary servanthood say to your life and circumstances? Wait patiently, listen expectantly, and obey swiftly.

❧ Paul says that love is not resentful and does not keep accounts (1 Cor. 13:5). If you have a serious problem with someone, write down on a piece of paper all of your "hurts"—both ways in which you have been hurt and ways in which you may have been hurtful. Then bring the list to God in prayer. Surrender the first half to him and ask forgiveness for the other half. Then burn the piece of paper as a helpful sign that God truly forgives, and that he will strengthen you to do the same.

✢ Begin each day for a week or two by asking God to lead you moment by moment into surrender to his will. Ask, "Lord, where do I plant myself today? In what acts of love? What routines of service? What words of witness and encouragement?"

✢ This week, follow the lead of St. Therese of Lisieux and look for the "little ways" to love and serve others. Do you have any enemies? Pray especially for them and find hidden ways to serve them. These acts will unite you with the humble heart of Jesus, who died at the hands of his "enemies" to bring all of us into new life.

✢ The pathway of humility is not easy. Review the areas of yielding above, then select an area to give special attention for the next few weeks. Make specific decisions and plans for practicing submission. Make a record of your attempts and share this with someone to whom you are accountable. What you do for a time in a focused and deliberate way, in dependence on the Holy Spirit, will eventually become natural and habitual.

9

Fasting

"Fasting? Are you serious? You gotta be kidding! What for?" Such statements are all too common among Christians in this age of instant gratification where feeling good and feeling full are idols of worship. Most people struggle to abstain from food—or anything else—for the sake of growing spiritually and drawing closer to God. At his previous church, Siang-Yang led a series of weekly meetings on spiritual practices. When he came to the topic of fasting, one church member asked if Siang-Yang was serious about practicing the spiritual discipline of fasting. The man had found the discussion of the topic interesting but had not considered fasting in his own life or in the lives of others in the church a discipline to be taken seriously and actually practiced on a regular basis! His response fell into the "you gotta be kidding" category.

More recently a colleague at Fuller Theological Seminary told Siang-Yang that while he was aware of people fasting for health reasons or to lose weight, he did not believe that Christians today practiced regular fasting. After hearing about some of Siang-Yang's experiences with this discipline, the man began including fasting as part of his own spiritual practice.

Fasting is a most tangible and practical way of surrendering to God and allowing the Holy Spirit more control in our lives. By giving up food—the very sustenance of life—during a fast, control over one's own existence is surrendered and offered to the Lord.

Fasting can bring new insight and breathe new life into our relationship with God. As is true of all the spiritual disciplines, fasting hoists the sails of the soul in expectation of experiencing the gracious presence and empowering of God's Spirit. But, as we shall see, fasting also provides a particular opening to the Spirit's power and a unique dimension to our spiritual lives that aids our growth into Christlikeness.

Fasting is usually understood as the voluntary and intentional denial of a normal and even necessary function, such as eating food. People fast for many purposes—to lose weight, to tame the desires of the flesh, as a work of penance, or to make a political statement—but the primary Christian motivation for fasting is to open oneself to God.

Through fasting, we give up our appetites for food and other things we hold too close or take for granted. As we take a break from the things that hold us, we give the Holy Spirit permission to change us so that we become appropriately disengaged from the world. Freed by the Holy Spirit from bondage to materialism, lusts, gluttony, and greed, we experience more self-control and take deeper joy in our experience of God.

If we are serious about growing in God, if we long for more of the Spirit's enabling power, if we want to taste more of the joy that comes in glorifying God, we should thoughtfully and earnestly enter into the discipline of fasting. Arthur Wallis makes the challenge clear:

> A new generation ... is arising. There is concern in the hearts of many for the recovery of apostolic power. But how can we recover apostolic power while neglecting apostolic practice? How can we expect the power to flow if we do not prepare the channels? Fasting is a God-appointed means for the flowing of His grace and power that we can afford to neglect no longer.[1]

The Work of the Spirit in Fasting

For Jesus, fasting seemed to be a corollary of other activities to which he gave high priority, including spiritual struggle, prayer, and evangelism. He was led into times of fasting by the Spirit. On one occasion Jesus was driven by the Spirit into the wilderness for forty days of fasting to be tested in preparation for public ministry (Mark 1:12).

To his disciples, Jesus said "when you fast" (Matt.6:16)—not *if* you fast; but *when* you fast. He seemed to take for granted that his disciples would fast according to the Spirit's leading on a given occasion. The Holy Spirit will call and direct us into times of fasting if we ask him to and if we become sensitive to his prompting. He will do so by revealing to us our *needs*—our need for more prayer, clearer guidance, or protection.

Jesus went without food and drink during sojourns in the wilderness, prior to temptation, when he rose early to pray in solitary locations (Mark 1:35), and as a result of ministering to those in need. He declared that he had food to eat of which his disciples were ignorant, referring to the "food" or strength he was given to fulfill his Father's purposes (John 4:31–34). Life-giving power flowed to Jesus from his surrender into intimacy with the Father.

God-centered fasting always has as its motive to create an opening for God's revelation and mercy. It is not to coerce God or change his mind. Our *doing something* does not condition God's response. His heart's desire is to extend mercy to his children according to his perfect will. All of our fasting, therefore, should be a "scriptural means whereby we are melted into a more complete realization of the purposes of the Lord in our life, church, community, and nation."[2]

Fasting should always have a purpose, but we must be careful not to elevate our purpose over his. In the church Doug pastored a few years ago, many in the congregation fasted for several days in preparation for important planning meetings and to support a heartfelt desire that God would cleanse the church from past sin and bring about the "something new" he seemed to be promising. During the time of fasting, the Holy Spirit showed Doug how much he had been pressing on the church his own ideas about the future, so much so that he was in danger of missing the "new thing" God was preparing. Doug realized that his thinking needed readjusting, and he asked the Holy Spirit to reveal his will regarding the matters at hand. Through this encounter, Doug was melted into a more complete realization of the purposes of the Lord in his life and the life of the church and surrounding community.

The Purpose of Fasting

Scripture reveals to us many spiritually motivated purposes for fasting. This helps us see how fasting is a spiritual discipline that aids us in our search for "all the fullness of God" (Eph. 3:19). Fasting in the Bible is never a means to "twist God's arm" to satisfy our desires. Rather it is a sign of a heart hungry for God. The Holy Spirit can touch our lives and draw us closer to the heart of God when we fast for the right reasons.

Fasting Strengthens Prayer

Often in the Bible, fasting occurs when there is a special urgency in prayer. Daniel "turned to the LORD God and pleaded with him in prayer and petition, in fasting," because of the great desolation that had come upon Jerusalem. Fasting sharpened the edge of Daniel's intercession and gave passion to his cry for God to listen, forgive, and act (Dan. 9:3, 17–19). The church at Antioch, "after they had fasted and prayed," sent Paul and Barnabas off on the first missionary journey (Acts 13:3). John Calvin thought that whenever someone was to approach God about a great matter "it would be expedient to appoint fasting along with prayer."[3]

David Brainerd, eighteenth-century missionary to Native Americans in New England, fasted during seasons of intercession as preparation for his ministry of preaching the gospel. He found that through fasting, God drew near and richly blessed him as he wrestled ardently in intercession for "absent friends, for the ingathering of souls, for multitudes of poor souls ... in many distant places."[4] Siang-Yang fasts one meal a week and has been blessed in this practice with more time for prayer, greater intimacy with God, and empowerment by the Spirit to pray more intensely for others.

Fasting Enables Us to Better Hear the Voice of God

When we fast, our spirits are focused and more concentrated on listening for what God is saying, and we are able to hear and receive clear guidance. Daniel received a vision from God after fasting (Dan. 10:2–3), the Spirit guided the church at Antioch after fasting to set Barnabas and Paul aside for missionary work, and Paul and Barnabas prayed and fasted to receive God's guidance before appointing elders in the churches they founded (Acts 14:23).

Fasting Aids Us in Self-denial and Self-discipline

The apostle Paul compares the Christian life to an athlete who exercises self-control and self-discipline in order to win the race (1 Cor. 9:26–27). "I afflicted myself with fasting," cries King David (Ps. 35:13 NRSV). Fasting is a way of attaining self-control over our natural desires.

Dietrich Bonhoeffer, a twentieth-century German pastor martyred by the Nazis in 1945, found great value in fasting. He wrote, "Fasting helps to discipline the self-indulgent and slothful will which is so reluctant to serve the Lord, and it helps to humiliate and chasten the flesh."[5] Bonhoeffer is not referring here to some kind of masochistic indulgence or ostentatious asceticism. He is referring to clear biblical teaching that we should maintain some self-control over our bodies, even to the point of denying ourselves certain necessities or pleasures for a time, in order to surrender to God and train for the service of Christ.

Doug does not fast on a regular basis, but when he does fast he realizes how generally unaware he is of his dependence on meals and snacks and other pleasures for his well-being. Fasting helps him to become aware of and to evaluate areas in his life that are out of control and are hindering him from surrender to God and sensitivity to the Holy Spirit.

Fasting Helps Us Face Persecution

King Jehoshaphat, when notified that a great army was coming against him, proclaimed a fast for all Judah (2 Chron. 20:3–4).

Queen Esther asked her uncle Mordecai to "gather together all the Jews who are in Susa, and fast for me" for protection from the king's wrath (Est. 4:16). Donald Whitney asserts:

> Fasting, rather than fleshly efforts, should be one of our first defenses against "persecution" from family, schoolmates, neighbors, or coworkers because of our faith. Typically we're tempted to strike back with anger, verbal abuse, counter accusations, or even legal action. But instead of political maneuvering, gossiping, and imitating the worldly tactics of our enemies, we should appeal to God with fasting for protection and deliverance.[6]

Fasting helps us, when we face opposition, to maintain perspective and to continue in the path God has set before us. As we fast, the Holy Spirit will help us to handle persecution in a more Christlike way.

Fasting Is a Way of Humbling Ourselves Before God

The people of Israel, under the judge Samuel, fasted and confessed their sin against the Lord (1 Sam. 7:6). The Ninevites humbled themselves before God and fasted in response to the word of the Lord from Jonah that their city would be overturned in forty days (Jonah 3:5). When Paul was struck blind in his encounter with Jesus on the road to Damascus, he humbled himself before the Lord, taking no food or water for three days, before God restored his sight and filled him with the Holy Spirit (Acts 9:8–9, 18).

Fasting reinforces the seriousness of a matter, showing through our actions as well as our words that our hearts are broken and our repentance sincere. Though we can in no way pay the penalty for our sins through fasting—Christ has already done that on the cross—entering into a time of fasting can be a gesture of submission and surrender to God, telling him that we too feel the pain of our sins. In fasting, we humble ourselves before God, acknowledging our dependence upon him for strength and power to respond in new righteousness and obedience.

Fasting Strengthens Us Against Temptation

Jesus fasted for forty days and forty nights, and in the spiritual strength that he experienced, he overcame the temptations of the devil and submitted himself solely to his Father's power and purpose for the public ministry just ahead of him (Matt. 4:1–11). Jesus' example teaches us that fasting is a means of helping us to have victory over temptation and to dedicate ourselves afresh to God for his service.

Many Christians have testified how, through fasting and prayer, they have experienced victory over particular sins and broken long-term bondage or addictions in their lives. A pastor friend of Siang-Yang fasts regularly for strength in overcoming temptations of lust and pornography. Fasting greatly weakens these temptations, which have overwhelmed him in the past. The powerful presence of Christ that comes through fasting strengthens Siang-Yang's friend in winning the battles and walking in victory.

Fasting Helps Us Minister to the Needs of Others

The kind of fasting God wants us to practice should lead to caring for others and meeting their needs, especially those who are oppressed, hungry, or poor. "Is not this the kind of fasting I have chosen:" says the Lord, "to loose the chains of injustice and untie the cords of the yoke, to set the oppressed free and break every yoke? Is it not to share your food with the hungry and to provide the poor wanderer with shelter—when you see the naked, to clothe him, and not to turn away from your own flesh and blood?" (Isa. 58:6–7). We are not to separate our inner spiritual lives from our outward actions.

We resonate with God's heart when we give the food we would have eaten to the poor, or the money that a meal would have cost to the homeless. For Jesus, spirituality was not relegated to the interior life; he was in solidarity with the poor and needy. When we fast as a means of identifying with the poor, we are living out the incarnational ministry of Jesus: "Whatever you did for one of the least of these brothers of mine, you did for me" (Matt. 25:40).

Fasting Helps Us Express Love and Worship to God

Fasting may be an act of pure adoration and worship to God. Anna "never left the temple but worshiped night and day, fasting and praying" (Luke 2:37). She knew Jesus' destiny while he was yet in his mother's womb! We can be so caught up into the love of God, so lost in adoration of his beauty and holiness, that we have no appetite and no concern for food. As we change our focus from food and material wants to God and eternal realities, there comes a rhythm of preference for the spiritual feast over the edible.

Fasting must always be God-centered. When fasting, thoughts of food should direct us to thoughts of God. Instead of distracting us, thinking of food should remind us of our purpose in fasting— to draw near in surrender to God. Jesus says that when we fast, we are not to be like hypocrites seeking the praise of others and honor for ourselves. Rather, Jesus tells us to fast in secret so that our fasting is obvious "only to your Father, who is unseen; and your Father, who sees what is done in secret, will reward you" (Matt. 6:18).

And what is the reward? More of God! Jesus is calling for a radical orientation on God himself. He is pressing us to have a real, authentic, personal relationship with God. If God is not real to us, fasting will be a miserable exercise that reduces us to self-justification, just like the hypocrites wanting the praise of others. When our relationship with God is real, then fasting brings entry into his gracious presence, reminder of his tender love and provision, renewal of passion, and desire that his kingdom come and his will be done on earth as it is in heaven (Matt. 6:10).

The response of God to our fasting is full of grace, mercy, and power. It is God who acts and moves. The victory in battle is the Lord's. Guidance, vision, and prophecy come from God. Protection from enemies is by the hand of the Lord, and the staying of destruction is due to God's mercy. We have fasted, but it is God who is at work. As he extends divine mercy, favor, and power, our hearts are melted and our willingness to surrender deepened. Our natural response is to praise and worship him, to give him our thanksgiving and obedience.

The Practice of Fasting

Several kinds of fasts are described in the Bible: There is a *partial fast*, which is a restriction of diet instead of total abstention from food, as with Daniel who did not eat choice food, meat, or wine for three weeks (Dan. 10:3). There is also a *normal fast* from eating food (while drinking liquids), which is dramatically illustrated in Jesus' forty days and forty nights of fasting in the desert, after which he was hungry (Matt. 4:2). And occasionally there is an *absolute fast* from all food and water, as is the case with Paul shortly after his conversion experience (Acts 9:9). In addition there are *regular fasts*, such as on the Day of Atonement (Lev. 16:29–31), and *corporate fasts* (Joel 2:15–16; Acts 13:2).[7]

The most common discipline of fasting among Christians has been a normal fast of abstaining from food for a day or two while drinking water and fruit juice. Recently, Bill Bright, founder of Campus Crusade for Christ, undertook a normal fast of forty days. He believes the Lord is calling millions of Christians to a similar fast for spiritual awakening in America and around the world before the year 2000:

> America and much of the world will, before the end of the year 2000, experience a great spiritual awakening. This divine visit of the Holy Spirit from heaven will kindle the greatest spiritual harvest in the history of the church. But before God comes in revival power, the Holy Spirit will call millions of God's people to repent, fast and pray.[8]

Fasting is still a new practice for most of us, and a forty-day fast may sound impossible and even terrifying, but once we have entered into fasting, we can trust the Holy Spirit to grow us into this discipline in a way that is honoring to God and renewing for ourselves.

We suggest starting with a one- to two-day normal fast. Here are some practical tips to review as you begin:

- Be sure you are not suffering from any medical condition (e.g., diabetes, ulcers) that would cause danger to you if you fasted. If you are unsure, you should consult your physician for medical advice before proceeding with a fast.

- Remember, the primary purpose of fasting is to seek the Lord. God must be your focus throughout the day. Review the biblical purposes for fasting outlined in the previous section.
- Ask the Spirit to reveal the kind of fast God wants you to undertake (e.g., partial fast, water only for one to two days, or a longer fast of a week or more).
- Prepare your heart by meditating on verses related to fasting (Matt. 4:2–11, 6:16–18; 2 Chron. 7:14; Joel 1:14; Dan. 9:3–19; Zech. 7:5–7). Allow the Holy Spirit to search your heart and lead you into any necessary confession and repentance.
- Eat a light meal before beginning your fast. Eating a big meal will only increase your hunger later.
- Hunger pangs are normal. To ease them, slowly sip water or fruit juice. The pangs will soon pass.
- If you are a regular coffee or tea drinker, you might experience a headache. This will also pass.
- Use the times you usually eat a meal for conversation with God, intercession, and reading Scripture.
- Consider also "fasting" from regular television viewing, newspaper reading, or shopping. This will help you keep your focus clear throughout the day.
- It is normal to feel weak or tired at some point during the fast. You may need to rest or take a short nap to renew your energy.
- Expect spiritual attack! Satan knows the power of fasting and prayer. You may be tempted to break the fast before the time is up. Ask the Holy Spirit to help you to persevere.
- Break your fast with a light meal. During the fast your stomach has shrunk, so eating a heavy meal can cause discomfort.[9]

What can you expect during and after a fast? Below is a first-hand account of a student's first attempt at fasting—a two-day fast from solid food that included fasting from coffee and from watching television. His primary purpose in fasting was "to hear from God at a time when I was very concerned about future direction, vocation, and ministry."

On the first day, I found myself to be a little hungry by mid-morning, even though I usually do not eat breakfast. However, I usually drink coffee in the morning and I think I felt this lack. . . . By the afternoon, I was not too hungry, but I was developing a headache. I pulled out [some notes] on fasting to find out what I had gotten myself into. I ran into a few "I told you so" parts: "You may experience headaches during this time, especially if you are an avid coffee or tea drinker." Aha! Yet I felt confident that I was engaged in something that was very much focused on God and not on my own accomplishment. I was totally dependent on the Lord to lead me through the fast.

By evening, my headache was nearly incapacitating, but I felt better after a short nap. I was able to complete some reading of *The Imitation of Christ* [by Thomas à Kempis] and found myself to be surprisingly attentive. The next morning, the headache was gone and throughout the day I did not feel hungry at all. I was very happy that I chose to continue the fast for the second day because I was now really feeling the benefits of devotion to God. I devoted the entire afternoon to prayer and reflection while my wife was out with a friend. It was an excellent time of experiencing thankfulness for everything that God has provided for me, of feeling that I could trust God with my future without fear, and of knowing that God was not far from me in the difficult times of my life but was and is really always present and caring. I think I was able to understand in a fresh way what it means to have your heart filled with the Spirit. I also saw how different practices of mine, like watching television, could crowd out the Spirit and make it difficult for me to be sensitive to God's calling and leading.

... The next day I had a fantastic experience I feel directly resulted from my time of fasting. I felt for the first time in a long while that the Holy Spirit was within me. It was such a good feeling that I believe that I now understand why many devoted Christians like Brother Lawrence and Thomas à Kempis desired nothing else than to be close to God.... I felt as if my eyes and ears had been opened in the manner of the Isaiah 6:9–10 passage.... I had a deeper and more profound understanding of the love of God. This is not surprising, I suppose, since the intent of fasting is to draw us closer to God.[10]

Fasting from Other Things or Activities

Fasting can also be seen in its broader context as a voluntary denial of an otherwise normal activity for spiritual reasons. As Oswald Chambers says: "Fasting from food is an easy business, but fasting in its true nature means to fast from everything that is good until the appointments of God in my soul are accepted."[11]

We surrender to God whenever we give up a regular activity in order to be more attentive to his presence and receptive to his will and purpose. For example, when we enter into solitude and silence (see chapter 3), we are "fasting" from interaction with people. Many of us are so busy with our schedules and occupied with personal relationships we have little time and space for listening and reflection. We love people best and interact with them in the most caring ways when we sometimes stay away and receive replenishment of "living water" from our Lord. Fasting from relationships provides a needed balance to many of our lives.

It is most helpful, for most of us, to regularly fast from the all-pervasive mass media of our culture—newspapers, radio, television, billboards, pulp fiction, and magazines. Some of us cannot get through the day without turning on the radio or television.

Information from the media, which sends us many false voices and noises, often drowns out God's voice. We will be able to hear the still, small voice of God more clearly as we surrender to him and ask the Spirit to free us from bondage to the media.

It is also helpful for us to take a break from the very things we most take for granted. Doug once challenged a student, the son of a wealthy doctor, to try to get along for two weeks on only ten dollars. The money was gone in a few days. He had no money for those "extra" snacks he was used to, he couldn't go to the Friday night movie or buy a compact disc he coveted, and he was reduced to borrowing money from a friend to buy gas for his car in order to keep a necessary commitment. He had never been dependent on others for that kind of help, and it brought shocking awareness to him of the power and control exerted through money. At the end of two weeks, he was on a different journey in his self-understanding and his need for dependence on God.

Finally, most of us could benefit by fasting from our gluttonous consumer culture—our tendency to buy more and more things. As we fast from such spending and buying, we can use the time and money saved to visit and bless the broken, the bruised, and dispossessed. We will see Christ in their faces and learn from him through them.

Andrew Murray believed that "fasting helps to express, to deepen and to confirm the resolution that we are ready to sacrifice anything, to sacrifice ourselves to attain what we seek for the Kingdom of God."[12] While fasting is not a familiar and easy discipline that most of us practice on a regular basis, it is an important means for us to receive God's grace and for the Holy Spirit to do his transformation work in us, drawing us closer to the heart of God.*

* Many of the ideas in this chapter were taken from Donald Whitney's book *Spiritual Disciplines for the Christian Life*, Chapter Nine. Copyright 1991. Used by permission of NavPress Publishing, Colorado Springs, CO 80935.

Entering In

If you get anxious even thinking about missing a meal, ask the Holy Spirit to give you perspective and call you into the discipline of fasting. You have probably thought nothing about missing a meal while shopping, working, playing sports, or trying to lose weight, so don't get anxious about missing a meal or two for the sake of becoming more like Jesus. Remember that at times it is not only more important, but also much more rewarding, to feast on God rather than on food.

Right now:

Plan a fast of dedication as an expression of surrender to God and of your willingness to fast in the future. As long as there are no medical reasons to keep you from fasting from food, commit yourself in prayer to fast once this week by skipping one or two meals, setting aside the time saved for prayer and rededication to God. Share with God your heart's desire to know him, love him, and serve him. Expect the Holy Spirit to help you to surrender and draw near through your fast.

In the coming days and weeks:

❧ Continue to experiment with a one- or two-meal fast. Be aware of any rationalizations you grab hold of to avoid fasting; they will teach you much about yourself. Look for ways to experience God's grace through fasting. Remember that God commanded every Israelite to fast for one whole day each year on the Day of Atonement (Lev. 16:29–31). If God thought it was good for them, perhaps it will be good for you too. To give you encouragement, reread the story above of the student's first experience of fasting.

❧ Ask the Holy Spirit to guide you into a regular rhythm of fasting—once a week, perhaps, for one or two meals. Continue to use the time in communion with God, in prayer, and in reading Scripture. You might also spend part of the time interceding for others.

❧ Try a "normal fast"—perhaps during a silent retreat—of two to three days, surrendering yourself to God, asking the Holy Spirit to convict you of sin and lead you to repentance and closeness to God. Take time for God to hold you in his loving arms—like the good shepherd filled with joy at finding and holding his wayward sheep. Pour out your heart's pains and desires to him.

❧ If the Holy Spirit leads you, try a period of fasting from three to seven days, but only from solid food. Make sure you drink plenty of water and juices, and if need be, even some soup or broth. Enter into and end such longer fasts gradually. You can give the money you save from not eating several meals to ministries that meet the needs of the poor, hungry, and homeless. If you feel led by God to explore a much longer time of fasting, perhaps for forty days, you might want to read Bill Bright's book *The Coming Revival—America's Call to Fast, Pray, and Seek God's Face* and ask the Holy Spirit if he is calling you into such a time of fasting.

❧ Try fasting for a day or even a week or more from something such as people, money, television, radio, movies, car, telephone, or shopping, that holds you in its grip and compromises your relationship with God. Be sensitive to what the Holy Spirit wants to say to you as you fast from the noise and hurry of the world. Journal about what you are hearing and learning from God's still, small voice during this time.

10

Worship

Worship is "lovemaking" with God. The most common New Testament word for worship—*proskuneo*—literally means to "step towards to kiss." We can bow and prostrate ourselves before God from a distance, but we must be close, intimate, trusting, and vulnerable if we are to step forward into God's loving embrace and receive his kiss of life, his Holy Spirit. Worship, properly speaking, is our response of love to the God who has reached out in love to us. "It is quite impossible to worship God without loving Him," writes A. W. Tozer, "and the inward operations of the Holy Spirit will enable us ... to offer Him such a poured-out fullness of love."[1]

In worship we come face-to-face with the living God, beholding him as he really is, letting our hearts assume their rightful place in response to him. God desires to reveal himself to us. When we come before him believing that "he exists and that he rewards those who earnestly seek him" (Heb. 11:6), we can expect that he will impress upon our thoughts, feelings, and understanding, by his Spirit, true knowledge of himself. In this "seeing" or "beholding" of him, all our self-righteousness, all our pretense, even all our "goodness" is seen for what it really is. We know that he is God, and we are not. Our only possible response, when we behold him face-to-face, is to worship him—giving ourselves over to him in trust and in surrender to his love.[2]

In 1982, at a point of transition in his life and crying out for more of God, Doug went to a weekend pastors' conference. Dur-

ing the weekend, the Holy Spirit led him to confess, over breakfast with some friends and colleagues, a previously unconfessed sin
about which he was deeply ashamed. A huge burden was lifted off
him and during the rest of that day he increasingly felt the love
and presence of the Lord, and new freedom and release of the
Spirit in his whole being. In the middle of the afternoon session,
Doug felt strongly that he should be on his knees before God.
Since he was sitting in an aisle seat, he quietly slipped to his knees.
Then, somehow, he caught a glimpse of the glory of the Father. In
Doug's own words:

> For just a mini-second, the Spirit opened a window in my
> spirit, and I was undone by what I saw. It happened so fast
> that I could not have told you at the time what I actually
> saw, but the response of my whole being was immediate.
> With my face buried in the carpet, I was crying at the top of
> my voice, "Oh God! Oh God! Oh God!" again and again. I
> was worshiping at his feet, like Peter, declaring myself to be
> a sinful man (Luke 5:8). The speaker, who had stopped in
> the middle of his talk, pointed to me lying prostrate on the
> floor and said, "Now see, that's the only way you can pray
> that prayer!" During the following thirty minutes, I was lost
> in worship; I could do nothing else. I was content to reflect
> back to God the radiance of his glory; to declare his mar-
> velous worth—"You are worthy, our Lord and God, to
> receive glory and honor and power" (Rev. 4:11). God's Spirit
> had touched my spirit and I was surrendered to his arms, lost
> in his love, aware of his healing, humbled by his forgiveness,
> overcome by his promises. All my pride, fear of embarrass-
> ment, self-righteousness, need for affirmation, and striving
> for importance was like so much chaff blown away by the
> wind of the Spirit, leaving behind the seed of possibility—
> my surrendered self—through whom God could do great
> things. There was nothing I had to do or perform; I was con-
> tent to belong to him and trust him to grow me more into
> his likeness.

Worship is our deepest act of surrender. It is meant to be intimate, personal, and all-consuming. In worship, when Spirit touches spirit, God's life is imparted to us, his imprint is left upon us, and we carry ever more clearly the Spirit-imparted pattern of adopted sons and daughters. Glorifying and praising God, giving him his worth, is the very best thing for us as human beings. We are made to worship the almighty God; meant to be transformed through worship into his likeness.

Do you want to be more like Jesus, who is "the radiance of God's glory and the exact representation of his being?" (Heb. 1:3). Then "fix your thoughts on Jesus, the apostle and high priest whom we confess" (Heb. 3:1). We become like that upon which we focus. We begin to be transformed into the likeness of that which gains our attention. "Let us fix our eyes on Jesus, the author and perfecter of our faith" (Heb. 12:2). As we worship God in the freedom the Spirit gives, we reflect the Lord's glory and are being "transformed into his likeness with ever-increasing glory, which comes from the Lord, who is the Spirit" (2 Cor. 3:17–18).

Worshiping in Spirit and in Truth

True worshipers," said Jesus, "will worship the Father in spirit and truth, for they are the kind of worshipers the Father seeks. God is spirit, and his worshipers must worship in spirit and in truth" (John 4:23–24).

Jesus spoke these words across the gender, cultural, and racial barriers of his day to an adulterous Samaritan woman, in a situation where no good Jewish teacher would be caught dead. Hot, tired, and thirsty, in the midst of mundane daily life and faced with this least likely prospect, Jesus was inviting this woman of Samaria to be a worshiper of the Father "in spirit and in truth." She wanted to know "where" such worship should take place; Jesus wanted her to know that *how* and *whom* she worshiped were more important. Worship must be "in spirit," vital and real in the heart, and it must be "in truth," based on a true perception of God. Worship must have heart and head; it must engage emotions and thought.[3]

How do we worship? In spirit! We need the Holy Spirit to make worship genuine and Spirit-filled. When Spirit touches spirit, we come alive in our emotions and inner devotion. Paul said that Christians worship by the Spirit of God (Phil. 3:3). The Spirit gives us a sense of the reality and presence of God as he takes the things of Christ and the Father and shows them to us (John 16:14–15). By the Spirit, our hearts come alive with passion for Christ; we are plugged in, there is electricity for worship. The Holy Spirit witnesses with our spirit that we are children of God, prompting us to cry "Abba! Father!"

Who do we worship? The one true God. Without the Holy Spirit, whose name is "Spirit of truth" (John 14:17), true worship will not happen. The Spirit of truth directs our hearts to pray and praise in full harmony with the truth about God, revealed in his Word. God is holy, and we worship him in the splendor of holiness (Ps. 29:2; 96:9). God is love, so we are to love him with all our heart and soul and strength. The Holy Spirit reveals God to us and makes Christ irresistible. In true worship we turn from every other god—any person, thing, ambition, or desire—that is granted first place in our hearts, and yield absolute trust to the one true and living God.

Worshiping in spirit alone would lead to purely emotional worship, marked by frenzy and a grasping after exciting experience and emotional highs. Worshiping in truth alone would lead to purely intellectual worship, falling into dead formalism and lifeless affirmation of orthodoxy. Real worship holds these two elements together: (1) a true vision of the greatness, goodness, holiness, and beauty of God; and (2) human spirits ignited by the Holy Spirit with fire, passion, and love for God. Heart *and* head! In this way, we will be changed, transformed from one degree of his likeness into another, released in both emotion and thought into powerful worship—into confessions, longings, acclamations, tears, songs, shouts, bowed heads, lifted hands, and obedient lives.[4]

Julian of Norwich, the fourteenth century English mystic, experienced great joy in contemplation of her lover, Jesus. Her whole life, which she summarized as a desire for "oneing with

God" was a continuing love affair marked by worship in spirit and truth. She fixed her eyes on Jesus and let nothing else come in the way. "Our lover," she wrote, "desires indeed that our soul should cleave to him with all its might, and ever hold on to his goodness." She thought the love of God for us to be so wonderful that no created being could ever know the greatness, sweetness, and tenderness of that love. "By his grace and help," she challenged, "let us in spirit stand and gaze, eternally marvelling at the supreme, surpassing, singleminded, incalculable love that God, who is goodness, has for us. Then we can ask reverently of our lover whatever we will. For by nature our will wants God, and the good will of God wants us. . . ."[5]

The Work of the Spirit in Worship

The Spirit fills us with power to worship. Paul, following his exhortation to the Ephesians to "be filled with the Spirit," begins to describe worship as the natural and inevitable overflow from the Spirit's filling. Instead of getting drunk on wine, which leads to debauchery, be filled with the "new wine" of the Spirit which overflows into worship: "Speak to one another with psalms, hymns and spiritual songs. Sing and make music in your heart to the Lord, always giving thanks to God the Father for everything, in the name of our Lord Jesus Christ" (Eph. 5:18–20). A closer look at this verse reveals several things about the filling of the Holy Spirit.

The first sign of the Spirit's filling is spiritual fellowship. As the Spirit works in us we are able to encourage one another through shared worship.[6] We are to speak to one another not in worldly chitchat but in "psalms, hymns, and spiritual songs." Corporate worship often begins with a call to the people to sing unto the Lord. The natural beginning of our glorifying God is to speak to one another through a psalm or hymn, exhorting one another to give God the glory due his name (Ps. 105:1–4).

The Holy Spirit also enables us to praise God wholeheartedly. A second sign of the Spirit's fullness is to "sing and make music" to the Lord. The Holy Spirit loves to glorify, exalt, and magnify the

Lord Jesus Christ (John 15:26; 16:14), manifesting him to us in such a way that we delight to sing his praises and offer him our service of worship. Praise and worship should be "in your heart"—or "with all your heart" (RSV)—and "to the Lord." The Spirit sets us free for heartfelt and heart-expressed worship. Says David Hubbard:

> He sets us free to praise God, to celebrate his deeds, to adore his name. Free from the distractions of our own needs, free from the tensions of our society, free from the tedium and pressure of life itself, we focus on the greatness and goodness of God—the God who can meet our needs, support us in the tensions, raise us above the tedium, steady us amid the pressures.[7]

Finally, flooding our experience with God's love and peace, the Holy Spirit helps us to give thanks always and in everything in Christ's name. A third sign of the Spirit's working worship in and through us is when we are able to give thanks in everything. It's easy for most of us to give thanks some of the time, and for some things; but a mark of the Spirit's work is that the believer gives thanks "to God the Father" in *all* things, "in the name of our Lord Jesus Christ." Grumbling and complaining are usually signs of unbelief, of distrust in God and doubt that "in all things God works for the good of those who love him" (Rom. 8:28).

Moaning and groaning—focusing on ourselves and our circumstances instead of on Jesus and his promises—is a sure sign of the Spirit's absence. Giving thanks for God's love and goodness—even in the middle of the most difficult circumstances—is a sure sign that the Holy Spirit is present. Paul is an outstanding example of one who gave thanks in everything (1 Thess. 5:16, 18). From a prison cell in Rome, he wrote to the Philippians: "I have learned the secret of being content in any and every situation, whether well fed or hungry, whether living in plenty or in want. I can do everything through him who gives me strength" (Phil. 4:12–13).

The Holy Spirit keeps worship fresh. He blows where he wills and is always new and creative. When we "open a window" to the Spirit as we enter into worship, we can expect the Spirit to blow upon us and lead us in worship. This is risky if we don't like change—if we prefer to worship the way we have the last hundred years, or the last ten years, or last week. If we say, "This is how it worked before, so let's do the same thing again today," we will start to try to "make" it work, and worship will lose the freshness of the life of the Spirit. We must learn to follow the gentle nudgings of the Spirit; to stop everything else and follow him into times of praise, or waiting, or making an offering of ourselves. Whatever the Spirit is doing, we are invited to do with him. Then Spirit touches spirit, and worship is vital and alive.

The Liberating Power of Praise

Praise provides the best pathway into worship because it is so natural to our way of life. It is ingrained into our basic makeup to spontaneously praise whatever we value. For example, it is nearly impossible to view a stunning sunset, to participate in an exciting sporting event, to hear a beautiful symphony, or to attend a pulsating rock concert without giving an exclamation of pleasure, clapping wildly for an encore, or shouting at the top of our lungs.

As a young man, Siang-Yang experienced all of these emotions and was naturally drawn to praise and worship God while watching the sun set during late afternoon walks along the shore in his birth country of Singapore. Doug, as well, was overcome with awe when, as a student, he first saw Michelangelo's "Pieta," a marble sculpture of Mary holding the crucified Jesus, in St. Peter's Cathedral in Rome. He sat in stunned silence for a half hour and could talk of nothing else for days.

Another built-in desire we have is to share what we enjoy with others, so they too can enter into the experience and give due praise to what we have found so worthy. C. S. Lewis wrote that "praise almost seems to be inner health made audible."[8] It is an expression of inner strength to praise. If we truly value God, then we should be bursting with a desire to give expression to our feelings about God. *Hallelujah* means "Praise to the Lord!—Isn't he beautiful? Isn't he majestic? Isn't he wonderful? Hallelujah!"

Imagine the closing minutes in a championship football game. Your team is down by six points and the other team is about to kick a field goal that will give them an insurmountable nine-point lead. Suddenly, your team blocks the field goal, picks up the ball, and runs it in for a touchdown. A total reversal of the expected outcome! Do you sit there quietly with your hands in your lap? No way! You are shouting (and probably losing your voice), and clapping, and stomping your feet, and slapping the backs of people around you and giving everyone high-fives. You would go crazy if you were not allowed to give full expression to your joy and pleasure.

This same sort of thing is happening in Revelation 4–5 when the saints in heaven actually see the Lord seated on his throne. What had seemed to be certain defeat at the hands of Satan is now overcome. At the point when things looked most bleak, Jesus has come out of the grave and the death-dealing Cross has turned to triumphant resurrection life. The victory is won, and we are on the winning side, participating in the victory celebration. A shout of praise goes forth that rocks the heavens. The four living creatures cry out day and night, "Holy, holy, holy is the Lord God Almighty, who was, and is, and is to come," praising the one who sits on the throne and who lives for ever and ever (Rev. 4:6–9).

The twenty-four elders fall down, casting their golden crowns before him, saying, "You are worthy, our Lord and God, to receive glory and honor and power, for you created all things, and by your will they were created and have their being" (Rev. 4:10–11). Who do you suppose these elders are? The top saints? Perhaps Paul, or St. Francis, or Mother Teresa? Whoever they are, it's clear from their golden crowns and thrones that they have bragging rights. Yet these elders, overcome by the presence of God, cast their crowns at his feet, crowns that are, as Paul confesses, so much garbage compared to the worth of knowing Christ Jesus and being at his feet in worship.

Then a great multitude of angels joins the living creatures and elders—"numbering thousands upon thousands, and ten thousand times ten thousand"—praising him in a loud voice, "Worthy is the

Lamb, who was slain" (Rev. 5:11–12). Every creature in heaven and on earth and under the earth and in the sea is praising God, saying "to the Lamb be praise and honor and glory and power, for ever and ever" (Rev. 5:13). Wow! This is what we are made for, to be part of the heavenly chorus giving praise to the one who is worthy, who has won the victory for us!

If we aren't naturally expressing our praise and thanksgiving to God, then we haven't yet understood who he is and what he has done. We may be at the "big game" of corporate worship, but we don't see what has happened and are sitting quietly with our hands in our laps. To understand what heaven really means, says C. S. Lewis, "we must suppose ourselves to be in perfect love with God—drunk with, drowned in, dissolved by, that delight which, far from remaining pent up within ourselves as incommunicable, hence hardly tolerable, bliss, flows out from us incessantly again in effortless and perfect expression.... In commanding us to glorify Him, God is inviting us to enjoy Him."[9]

Praise, more than anything else, will lead us into the gracious presence of God. At the dedication of the temple in 2 Chronicles 5, the glory of the Lord filled the house of God when the people began to praise God with one united voice, saying, "He is good; his love endures forever." In 2 Chronicles 20, faced with a tremendous battle, God's people began to sing and praise the name of God, and God came down in power and gave them a mighty victory. In Acts 4 the disciples faced the first wave of opposition to the growing church. They praised God and prayed, reminding themselves of the sovereignty of God. "After they prayed, the place where they were meeting was shaken. And they were all filled with the Holy Spirit and spoke the word of God boldly" (Acts 4:31). In Acts 16, Paul and Silas were beaten, stripped, and thrown into prison. Placed in an inner cell, with their feet fastened in stocks, they prayed and sang hymns to God until, at about midnight, a violent earthquake shook the foundations of the prison, opening prison doors and releasing the prisoners from their chains.

As we worship and praise God, our vision of God and our expectancy grows. Intercessory prayer becomes more powerful, and we receive faith to ask that mountains be removed. Praise is also the true language of heaven now and forever (Rev. 4–5; 7; 15; 19). So praise is the meeting place of heaven and earth; it brings a breath of heaven into our own individual lives and worshiping fellowships.

Does all this talk about praise whet your appetite and get you in the mood for worship? Are you ready, yearning, excited to praise God? Then do so. Stop right now. Offer up to the Lord a sacrifice of praise. Read a psalm of praise; sing a hymn or a chorus of praise; let your heart flow out toward God. Fix your mind on Jesus, his glory and majesty, his beauty and strength.

As we praise and worship like this our vision of God brightens, our faith grows strong, our prayer becomes real. The Lord longs to be gracious to us, to show his compassion. He waits for us to wait upon him (Isa. 30:15, 18) that he might pour his love into our hearts through the Holy Spirit. When Spirit touches spirit, then praise, confession, petition, adoration, and intercession follow as we seek his face.[10]

The Transforming Power of Worship

When we receive God's overtures of love in worship, we begin to be transformed by his life imparted to us. Like a pregnant woman, we slowly begin to "swell" on the outside as our lives and character are changed due to his transforming love within. The fruit of his Spirit—love, joy, peace, patience, kindness, goodness, faithfulness, gentleness, and self-control (Gal. 5:22–23)—begins to show itself in our countenance, behavior, and character. When we enter the spiritual discipline of worship on a regular basis, the Holy Spirit transforms us.

First, through worship, the Holy Spirit redirects our focus onto God and away from ourselves. For instance, when Siang-Yang is praying or reading Scripture and becomes aware of God's presence, worship naturally bubbles up from his heart and adoration for God pours forth from his lips. He praises God for his goodness, holiness, and beauty. In such moments any self-righteousness, tendency to self-focus, or need for self-justification is washed away by the renewing power of the Holy Spirit.

Second, in worship, the Holy Spirit gives us fresh experiences of God's love and mercy. Through contemporary praise music—especially Scripture verses put to melody and sung directly to Jesus from the heart—both Siang-Yang and Doug have experienced fresh renewal in worship. In focusing our eyes on Jesus there is new freedom to stand, clap, kneel, raise hands, and approach God during worship for forgiveness, healing, and empowering. As we experience deeper heart-love for Jesus in worship, many of the traditional hymns and prayers of the church will come alive again as powerful expressions of our faith and hope in the living God.

Third, during worship, the Holy Spirit gives us direction for the future. He can speak to us more clearly because our spirits are more finely tuned to him. In the midst of heartfelt corporate worship, when God is enthroned and present in the praises of his people (Ps. 9:1–11; 22:3), the way is opened for deep conversation and communion with God. It was in the midst of a worship service that Doug had confirmation from the Holy Spirit to leave his part-time position as a parish pastor and accept a position at Fuller Seminary. The Lord gave him very specific reasons for the change and a clear sense of what he was calling Doug to do in his new setting. Worship is often a place of listening for us, as praise to God flows over and around us creating space, light, and openness to the Lord.

Fourth, in the midst of powerful praise and worship, the Holy Spirit reveals the presence of the Enemy and exposes his schemes and devises. When God is present, his enemies scatter and his foes flee before him (Ps. 68:1). The darkness is overcome by the light. Strongholds and bondages of the Enemy are broken and dismantled when God is magnified and glorified. Doug has found that during powerful times of praise and worship during weekend student conferences, the Spirit often reveals to participants the places where the Enemy has a foothold in their lives, and strengthens them to resist the Enemy's temptation in those areas where they have sinned in the past.

On one occasion, near the end of a lengthy worship session, Doug found a young man curled into a fetal position, filled with fear, unwilling to make eye contact with him. As they talked and prayed, the Holy Spirit guided the student to repent of sin patterns of unforgiveness, anger, and sexual immorality, and to refuse the Enemy's foothold of authority that had been gained through these patterns. As forgiveness and healing began to flow, the "garbage" was removed from the student's life, and the power of the Enemy was broken.[11] The most effective spiritual warfare happens not when we focus on the spirits of darkness, but when our focus is on God—his glory, holiness, beauty, truth, power, and dominion. Worship and praise to our mighty God brings release of light and revelation of truth. The battle and the victory belong to the Lord (2 Chron. 20:15).

Finally, through wholehearted worship, the Holy Spirit changes our hearts and leads us into obedient lifestyles. True spiritual worship, says Paul, is offering ourselves completely to God in every aspect of our lives (Rom. 12:1). Our obedience, our surrender to the will of God, becomes our act of worship. True worship inevitably changes us. We cannot praise God and gossip with the same mouth. We cannot worship with a neighbor and harbor resentment against that same person. We cannot raise hands to God and then use the same hands to devise evil. Worship changes us.

Entering In

We have been created to worship the most high God, redeemed for an eternity of lovemaking with our wooing bridegroom, filled with the Spirit to sing psalms, hymns, and spiritual songs to the Lord with thanksgiving in our hearts. Let us more and more, each and every day, be worshipers of the most high God, brides to our lover Jesus, growing into the likeness of Christ as we are surrendered through worship to his will and purpose. "Lead me, Holy Spirit, into loving relationship and willing surrender. Help me to love God and enjoy him forever, with all of my heart, mind, soul, and strength."

Right now:

Using the words of Frances Havergal's well-known hymn, surrender yourself to God in confession, adoration, and praise.

> Take my life and let it be
> Consecrated, Lord, to Thee
> Take my moments and my days;
> Let them flow in endless praise.
> Take my voice and let me sing
> Always, only, for my King.
> Take my lips, and let them be
> Filled with messages from Thee.
> Take my will and make it Thine;
> It shall be no longer mine.
> Take my heart, it is thine own;
> It shall be Thy royal throne.

Take my love; my Lord, I pour
At Thy feet its treasure store.
Take myself, and I will be
Ever, only, all for Thee.[12]

In the coming days and weeks:

- Make it a regular habit during the next few weeks to offer the Lord a "sacrifice of praise." As you pray, read the Bible, do the dishes, take a coffee break, or go for a walk, let your heart flow out toward God in praise. Let one or more of the psalms guide you as a starting point, or write your own psalm of God's grace to you and sing it to him. Fix your mind on Jesus, his glory and majesty, his beauty and strength. Let the Holy Spirit release in your spirit a language of praise. Remember that God invites us into his very self to taste and know his inner sweetness. Praise him for this and ask him to help you taste and know him more.

- Take some time this week to "hallow" God's name. His is the name above all names. He is God above all gods, the Lover of our souls, the Bridegroom, the Faithful One, Jesus, the Rock of Ages, King of the nations. Let the Spirit bring to your mind the names of God and the aspects of his character that these names reveal. Bless and praise him just for who he is yesterday, today, and forever.

- Take time to receive from the Spirit in worship. Lie still in a relaxing and comfortable place (bathtub, sofa, lawn chair, hillside) and listen to a favorite worship tape. Let the music and words wash over you, sinking into your head and heart. Be alert for those words and images the Holy Spirit wants to impress upon you. Imagine God singing one or more of these songs to you. Let your heart flow out toward God in surrender and thanksgiving.

- Imagine yourself in the throne room of God (Isa. 6; Rev. 4–5) worshiping with the seraphim, elders, and angels.

Feel the pillars of the temple shake from the loud praise. See the Lamb upon his throne and enter into vocal rejoicing and praise—"And he shall reign forever and ever . . . forever, and ever . . . alleluia, alleluia." Take your pride, accomplishments, and whatever concerns you have and cast them at his feet in surrender to him. He is worthy! Tell him so.

✞ As you attend corporate worship in the next few weeks, practice the presence of God on the way as a means of preparing your heart for worship. Some ideas: pray silently for those you see, thank God for the day and all its possibilities, ask him to bring to your mind things you should know about yourself or others. In this way, you are preparing your heart and mind to worship in spirit and in truth. Remember Paul's encouragement to be continually filled with the Spirit (which naturally overflows into worship) so that you are ready to enter into corporate worship with others, sharing psalms, hymns, and spiritual songs, making music in your heart to the Lord (Eph. 5:19–20).

IV

REACHING OUT
TO OTHERS:

Disciplines of Service

———

Each one should use whatever gift
he has received to serve others,
faithfully administering God's
grace in its various forms.

1 PETER 4:10

11

Fellowship

L et us consider how we may spur one another on toward love and good deeds," writes the author of Hebrews. "Let us not give up meeting together ... but let us encourage one another" (Heb. 10:24–25). Listen to these words again: *us, we, one another, together, encourage one another.* The Christian journey is fundamentally a shared journey. Christian life is a life of fellowship with others in Christian community.

J. I. Packer defines fellowship as "a seeking to share in what God has made known of himself to others, as a means to finding strength, refreshment, and instruction for one's own soul."[1] Such mutual challenge, growth, and edification is beautifully described by Paul in Ephesians 4:16, where he says, "the whole body, joined and held together by every supporting ligament, grows and builds itself up in love, as each part does its work." In Christian fellowship we become agents of the Holy Spirit in one another's growth and transformation, helping one another to surrender to God's will and reach out to others in loving service.

When Paul exhorts the Christians of Philippi to be like Christ, to have the mind of Christ, he gives this concrete description of what he means: "Do nothing out of selfish ambition or vain conceit, but in humility consider others better than yourselves. Each of you should look not only to your own interests, but also to the interests of others" (Phil. 2:3–4). Paul is saying that comparison, competition, and the tendency toward "go it alone" individual Christianity won't work and isn't good for us. Fellowship, esteeming others, helping one another—these are the marks of Christian discipleship. If our life in Christ means anything, if we take comfort from his love, if we have any fellowship with the Spirit, urges Paul, "then make my joy complete by being like-minded, having the same love, being one in spirit and purpose" (Phil. 2:1–2). Christians are to be united in love with a common purpose and common mind.

Jesus gathered the twelve disciples into a small community to share their lives with him and with each other. They lived every day with him—losing independence, gaining interdependence, benefiting from each other's strengths, helping to expose each other's weaknesses. They shared everything—joys, sorrows, dreams, defeats, possessions. They were called to depths of sharing, risk, and growth they had never known before.[2] For three years Jesus drew them into fellowship together, loved them, cared for their needs, explained the parables to them, modeled healing and prayer for them, sent them out to act on their faith, corrected them, guided them, prayed for them, and died for them. He laid down his life for his friends, and told them to do the same for each other (John 15:13–17).

So excited was the apostle John by the reality of the shared life the disciples enjoyed with Jesus—a reality available to all believers through Jesus' death, resurrection, and gift of the Spirit—that he began his first epistle with the words: "We proclaim to you what we have seen and heard, so that you also may have fellowship with us. And our fellowship is with the Father and with his Son, Jesus Christ" (1 John 1:3). All believers are invited into fellowship—into participation together in spiritual union with Christ. As we walk in truth and in the light, "we have fellowship with one another, and the blood of Jesus . . . purifies us from all sin" (1 John 1:7). David Watson writes:

> This sense of Christian community for all disciples was so strong and fundamental in the first century that salvation apart from the church was considered impossible. When individuals were added to the Lord, they were added to the church.

When they belonged to Christ, they belonged equally to his
body.... And since the New Testament concept of the church
is neither a building, an institution, nor an organization, but
the people of God, the disciples of Jesus were meant to gain
great strength from belonging to one another.[3]

We are so inclined in the West to think in terms of individualism and self-sufficiency that it is difficult to adjust our thinking—
and therefore our actions—to grasp and enter into the discipline
of true fellowship. When we enter into fellowship with Jesus
Christ, we enter into a new relationship with each other. Our relationship with Jesus and our relationship with one another can
never be separated. As Ron Sider summarizes, "The mind of Christ
is the mind that gathers us together in community; our life in community is the manifestation of the mind of Christ."[4]

We must be challenged again to examine the New Testament
materials and see the love and power that flowed from the early
Christian communities because of their fellowship with one
another. We must be ready to admit that by oneself it is nearly
impossible to defy the materialistic and individualistic pressures of
our society. God uses our brothers and sisters in Christ as a primary
means to transform us and help us to deal with our sin, sickness,
and cultural idolatries. The paralytic needed four friends to get him
to the place of healing. We need others with whom we can share
our weaknesses and strengths, who will support us, correct us, and
partner with us in mission and service. In the spiritual discipline of
fellowship, we help one another to grow out of pride, jealousy,
envy, competitiveness, and preoccupation with self. To be in community is a practical, concrete way to depend on the Holy Spirit
and grow in faith.

The Fellowship of the Holy Spirit

Genuine fellowship among believers is a result of the indwelling
presence of the Holy Spirit. In his closing salutation to the Christians at Corinth, Paul says, "May the grace of the Lord Jesus

Christ, and the love of God, and the fellowship of the Holy Spirit be with you all" (2 Cor. 13:14). Paul appeals to the Philippians to be one in spirit and purpose, in part because they share in "fellowship with the Spirit" (Phil. 2:1)—in spiritual union with Christ by the Holy Spirit. Paul declares that he wants "to know Christ and the power of his resurrection and the fellowship of sharing in his sufferings, becoming like him . . . to attain to the resurrection" (Phil. 3:10–11).

To the Romans and Corinthians, Paul speaks of the one body in Christ. "We were all baptized by one Spirit into one body . . . given the one Spirit to drink" (1 Cor. 12:13). We are to be a living organic reality which consists not of one member, but of many. We do not belong to ourselves, but to Christ. Every Christian is a necessary part of the body, and every Christian needs the help of every other Christian. Members are to care for one another, for if one member suffers, all suffer together, and if one is honored, all rejoice together (1 Cor. 12:14–27; Rom. 12:4–5).

A remarkable thing happened when the Holy Spirit came upon the disciples at Pentecost. During Jesus' earthly ministry, they had been divided, confused, fearful, jealous of one another, and filled with boastful pride. Then, in obedience to their risen Lord— who told them not to leave Jerusalem until they received the power of the Holy Spirit (Acts 1:4–8)—they joined in prayer and waited *together* for his promise to be fulfilled. When the Holy Spirit came, there was an explosion of loving fellowship that would be seen and heard around the world. Three thousand people were converted in one day (Acts 2:41).

Those who responded to the Apostles' teaching were quickly incorporated into shared fellowship: "All the believers were together and had everything in common. . . . Every day they continued to meet together in the temple courts. They broke bread in their homes and ate together with glad and sincere hearts, praising God and enjoying the favor of all the people" (Acts 2:44–47). There was such an explosion of love, freedom, joy, and power in the Spirit that people were being saved every day and being folded into an expanding network of household fellowships.

In Acts 4, Peter and John, having been released from arrest and told to stop speaking about Jesus, go to one of these home fellowships to share and pray and ask God for more boldness and power. "After they prayed, the place where they were meeting was shaken. And they were all filled with the Holy Spirit and spoke the word of God boldly" (v. 31). Lives were being transformed by the Holy Spirit through the power of fellowship. Ananias and Sapphira were exceptions. In their eagerness to look out for themselves, they held back from the Holy Spirit and lost their lives. In breaking fellowship, they were "dead" to the life-giving power of the Spirit (Acts 5:1–11).

The presence of God and the power of God's love in the fellowship of the first believers so amazed and surprised outsiders that they exclaimed, "See how they love one another." The power of the Holy Spirit was transforming lives through fellowships marked by love, sharing, accountability and evangelism, as they reached out in healing social ministry and service to touch the lives of those who came to see what they were about.

Doug often saw the power of this kind of fellowship during his years in college ministry. One fall, Christian students returned early to campus from a retreat where they had studied the first six chapters of the book of Acts. Arriving before the dorms opened, they camped out in three off-campus houses and practiced the kind of loving, caring, and sharing they had studied about in Acts 2 and 4. They slept together, about twenty to a household, in wall-to-wall sleeping bags. Trying to express their love and service, they were constantly saying to those around them things like, "You take the first shower," "No, you take the first shower," "I'll do the dishes," "Let me pay for that," or "Let me help you with that."

If their parents had been there to watch, they would have been incredulous! Love, so tangible and present in the relationships and fellowship of the students, was flowing out of them to those around them. Deep conversations were taking place. Everyone was of one mind and spirit in praying for new students and the new school year.

One evening there was a spontaneous birthday party for one of the students. Several people brought food and drinks, others provided dishes, utensils, music—each one sharing their gifts and resources. There were so many people, the party spilled outside the house and began to draw in neighborhood residents and attract other students who were returning to campus. It became a natural, powerful, pulsating, attractive event—with most of the conversations about God. No alcohol was present, just the power of love: "See how they love one another!"

Gathering together with fellow believers connects us with the power of the Holy Spirit. As we gather together in the name of Jesus to share, worship together, pray for healing and deliverance, receive guidance, hold one another accountable, confess to one another, extend forgiveness, and minister to one another's needs, we are in spiritual union with Christ—we are in the fellowship of the Holy Spirit, being transformed by the Holy Spirit into the character and likeness of Jesus.

The Power of Christian Fellowship

There is power in Christian fellowship. Christ works through his body. The Holy Spirit apportions gifts to each member of the body as he wills, "so that the body of Christ may be built up until we all reach unity in the faith and in the knowledge of the Son of God and become mature, attaining to the whole measure of the fullness of Christ" (Eph. 4:12–13). Spiritual gifts are given to each member for the common good. We are together to grow into the fullness of Christ from whom the whole body, in all its individual parts, grows in love and service (Eph. 4:16; 1 Cor. 12:7–26).

We cannot pursue the Christian adventure on our own. For growth to occur we need to love one another, submit to one another, learn from one another, and listen to one another and to what God may be saying to us through others. This is especially true in contemporary American culture where, as Ron Sider says,

The values of our affluent society seep slowly and subtly into our hearts and minds. The only way to defy them is to immerse ourselves deeply into Christian fellowship so that God can fundamentally remold our thinking, as we find our primary identity with other brothers and sisters who are also unconditionally committed to biblical values.[5]

First, there is transforming power in Christian fellowship. Under the power of the Holy Spirit, the early believers' lives were changed. They met together every day, eating together in their homes and praising God with glad and sincere hearts. "They devoted themselves to the apostles' teaching and to the fellowship, to the breaking of bread and to prayer. Everyone was filled with awe, and many wonders and miraculous signs were done" (Acts 2:42–43).

It has been traditional in the West to think "church" happens only on Sunday morning. But church is not only a building, and we are not a church only when we meet in a building. We are the church whenever and wherever we gather as believers. Today there are widespread efforts throughout the church to capture the quality of community life of the early church through establishing small groups, cell groups, or home fellowships for the purpose of encouragement, challenge, and equipping for ministry.

How can we spur on one another? Hebrews 10:24–25 tells us, "Let us consider how we may spur one another on toward love and good deeds.... let us encourage one another." Siang-Yang has been part of a small group from church who meet bi-weekly in his home. He has seen lives transformed through its fellowship. Participants often arrive tired and discouraged, thinking of all the reasons they don't have time for the meeting. Then, as they eat, share, study the Bible, and pray, energy begins to flow. They leave encouraged and reenergized, having been listened to, prayed for, and loved. "I'm so glad I came tonight," is their usual testimony to one another.

Two years ago Siang-Yang met a man at a checkout counter of a department store and, following a brief conversation, invited him to his small group. The man did, in fact, come to check out the group. He did not believe in God, but over the course of the next months, through sharing, receiving prayer, studying the Bible, and observing the group, he grew close to group members and to God. Before leaving town for a new job just recently he shared with the group that joining in the bi-weekly small group meeting had become one of the most meaningful things of his life. He had become less driven, more at peace, and more interested in God and in spiritual things. Through the life of the small home group, he had become a seeker after God.

Second, there is evangelizing power in Christian fellowship. The early believers, under the influence of the Holy Spirit, experienced such love, joy, and harmony of lifestyle and purpose that others were drawn to them like a magnet "and the Lord added to their number daily those who were being saved" (Acts 2:47). Explosive fellowship carried the Christian movement from 120 disciples on the Day of Pentecost to five thousand Christians in Jerusalem alone in a matter of months, and then planted the movement all over the known world in a few short decades.

When the gospel moves out of buildings and into homes and fellowship groups, it reaches people who might never come to a Sunday morning worship service. When church happens in the midst of a neighborhood, it's easy to reach out in loving service to others right from one's own living room. God has invited us to the banquet table! May we respond in such a way, welcoming others to join us, that many more families will stand beneath the fountain of his grace.

In a loving, sharing, community of God's people, newcomers sense something is alive and happening. They see joy and love, both visible demonstrations of God's presence. Doug is not certain of anyone who was converted to Jesus as a result of his teaching or preaching during his seventeen years as college chaplain, but he can name people who came to know God or were renewed in faith through the loving fellowship that gathered regularly for prayer, worship, Scripture study, and service. The challenge before us today is to be in such intimate fellowship with God and with one another that a watching world will be drawn to know Jesus through our witness.

Third, there is unifying power in Christian fellowship. The early chapters of Acts are filled with expressions of unity and oneness in Christ. The early Christians were all of one accord, praying together, holding all things in common, of one heart and mind, sharing everything. In C. S. Lewis's *Screwtape Letters*, the chief demon, Screwtape, tells his apprentice, Wormwood, that the philosophy of hell rests upon the simple axiom that one self is not another, and hence one self's good is not another's. Therefore, competition rather than shared community is the end of human existence. But Screwtape, quite perplexed, continues his letter:

> The enemy's [God's] philosophy is nothing more nor less than one continual attempt to evade this very obvious truth. He aims at a contradiction. Things are to be many, yet somehow also one. The good of one self is to be the good of another. This impossibility he calls Love.... Thus He is not content, even Himself, to be a sheer arithmetical unity; He claims to be three as well as one, in order that this nonsense about Love may find a foothold in His own nature. At the other end of the scale, He introduces into matter that obscene invention the organism, in which the parts are perverted from their natural destiny of competition and made to cooperate.[6]

Every area of our life as Christians is affected by our cooperation, our degree of unity in fellowship. "I tell you," says Jesus, "that if two of you ... agree about anything you ask for, it will be done for you by my Father in heaven" (Matt. 18:19). The word for agree, *sumphoneo*, means "in symphony with" or "in harmony with." Not just mental assent, but complete harmony in living with each other in love and forgiveness. If there is disharmony, bitterness, resentment, or jealousy, the power of fellowship is broken.

All great revivals and movements of the Holy Spirit have shown the power of unity. God promises to bestow his blessing whenever brothers dwell together in unity (Ps. 133). Jesus prayed to his Father, at the end of his earthly life, for all those who would believe in him through his disciples' message, that they would be one: "May they be brought to complete unity to let the world know that you sent me and have loved them even as you have loved me" (John 17:23). Jesus knew the power and love that would be released through unity among his followers.

Darrell Johnson, a pastor friend of ours, returned recently from a Promise Keepers event in Atlanta, Georgia—the largest and most diverse assembly of pastors in history. Fifty thousand pastors, representing nearly every denomination and association of churches and every cultural and ethnic background, gathered to find ways and means of bringing down the denominational and racial walls that presently divide the church of Jesus Christ. Max Lucado, one of the speakers, told the men there that the great sin of our time is not immorality of the nation, but the disunity of the church. Darrell's conclusion: This convention "is but one sign of the powerful move of the Holy Spirit we are witnessing in our time. I never thought I would actually get to see and experience it.... It's Ezekiel 37 right before our eyes!"[7]

Finally, there is purifying power in Christian fellowship. Being the kind of people who please God has more to do with being rightly related to one another than with simply doing the right things. We are called to be in relation with one another in a way that pleases God. Listen to his Word:

> Accept him whose faith is weak, without passing judgment on disputable matters.... Stop passing judgment on one another. Instead, make up your mind not to put any stumbling block or obstacle in your brother's way.... Nobody should seek his own good, but the good of others.... Speak truthfully to [your] neighbor, for we are all members of one body.... Do not let any unwholesome talk come out of your mouths, but only what is helpful for building others up, according to their needs, that it may benefit those who listen.... Get rid of all bitterness, rage and anger, brawling and slander, along with every form of malice. Be kind and compassionate to one another, forgiving each other, just as in Christ God forgave you.... Submit to one another out of reverence for Christ.... Bear with each other and forgive whatever grievances you may have against one another. Forgive as the Lord forgave you. And over all these virtues put on love, which binds them all

together in perfect unity (Rom. 14:1, 13; 1 Cor. 10:24;
Eph. 4:25, 29, 31–32; Eph. 5:21; Col. 3:13–14).

Living together in right relationship causes love and unity to
spring forth and draws the world's attention. Important questions
we must ask are: "What does the world see in us? Do we look different than the world? Have the values of our society, seeping
slowly and subtly into our hearts and minds, robbed us of the
transforming, evangelizing, unifying, purifying power of Christian
fellowship? Or are we, can we be, as Paul says, "blameless and pure,
children of God without fault in a crooked and depraved genera-
tion, in which [we] shine like stars in the universe as [we] hold out
the word of life" (Phil. 2:15–16)?

Healthy Christian Community

God's primary structure for helping us to deal with our sin and
sickness and cultural idolatries is each other. We are meant to be
in strong, healthy, loving communities of faith. We need others
who will support us, correct us, and partner with us in mission and
service. But genuine Christian community is difficult in a culture
which stresses individualism, self-sufficiency and competition in a
highly affluent and materialistic setting. We are in danger of being
"conformed to this world," of letting our culture squeeze us into its
own mold (Rom. 12:2 NRSV). In the discipline of fellowship we
receive help in growing out of pride, jealousy, envy, competitiveness, and self-centeredness.

There are three ingredients essential for healthy Christian
community: support, challenge, and common purpose.[8]

First, healthy Christian community provides support. In order
to grow, we need other people who will give us affirmation,
encouragement, care, unconditional love, and forgiveness. We
might call this "soft love," because it helps hold us together in fellowship. We all need people who love us, people with whom we
can be open and vulnerable.

True fellowship begins when we are free to be ourselves, free
to take off our masks and be honest with one another. When we

are willing to be open with others about our personal problems and needs—risking shock or rejection—and when we are willing for others to be equally open with us, we find ourselves together at the foot of the cross, the place of God's healing and grace. Paul says, "Accept one another, then, just as Christ accepted you, in order to bring praise to God" (Rom. 15:7). We know we are loved by God in Christ while we are still trapped in sin and brokenness. God's forgiving and caring love for us frees us to care and love others in the same manner.

Dietrich Bonhoeffer wrote out of his experience of community with young men training to be pastors: "When God was merciful to us, we learned to be merciful with each other. When we received forgiveness instead of judgment, we, too, were made ready to forgive our brethren. What God did for us, we then owed to others. The more we received, the more we were able to give.... Thus God himself taught us to meet one another as God has met us in Christ."[9]

When we meet one another as Christ has met us, our hearts remain soft, we forgive time and again, and the Spirit is dynamic in our midst.

Second, healthy Christian community requires challenge. Each of us needs accountability, correction, and good advice from others in order to grow. We can call this "tough love," because it helps mold us together in fellowship. Challenge from others provides a check on our bad habits and unhealthy actions. In a caring *and* challenging community, our motives and behavior can be questioned and reexamined. It enables us to break idolatries, throws us back into dependence on God, and creates a context for spiritual growth.

We are helped immeasurably in life by those who love us enough to give us honest feedback. Not too long ago, three of Doug's friends challenged him about a recurring pattern in his life of making enemies of those he believed had rejected him. They helped Doug see that he was often projecting motives and intentions on others that were not true. They reminded him of the way of Christ, who loved and prayed for his enemies and served those who did not understand him or rejected him. They helped Doug to return to walking once more on the path of esteeming others more highly than himself. As the proverb says, "Wounds from a friend can be trusted" (Prov. 27:6). We are to speak the truth to one another in love so that the whole body can be built up in love.

Paul charged Timothy to "preach the Word; be prepared in season and out of season; correct, rebuke and encourage—with great patience and careful instruction"—for this will help others to remain true to the gospel (2 Tim. 4:2). Bonhoeffer believed that "God has willed that we should seek and find his living Word in the witness of a brother.... Therefore, the Christian needs another Christian who speaks God's Word to him. He needs him again and again when he becomes uncertain and discouraged, for by himself he cannot help himself without belying the truth."[10]

The third ingredient for healthy Christian community is a common purpose—a shared vision for mission and outreach. It is vital that members of a community be involved together in ministry and service that provide direction, give shape, and create growth for the fellowship. Thus Paul affirms that the purpose of a body of believers is to bring every member into full maturity of faith, "attaining to the whole measure of the fullness of Christ" (Eph. 4:13).

Strong partnership, rooted in shared mission, keeps a group from becoming ingrown and cliquish. It encourages outreach to others. Without common vision, individuals in a fellowship vie for control and dominance. They are trapped in a merciless cycle of competition and performance that can only be broken by a common, biblically based vision of God's purposes.

The goal of all Christian community, says Bonhoeffer, is for us to "meet one another as bringers of the message of salvation."[11] The greatest blessings come when we move beyond a "what's in it for me?" attitude to one of giving our life away for others. Only then is life truly gained!

If there is to be a Christian presence that is salt and light, then there must be communities of Christians that are conformed to God and not to the world. Nothing is more needed in our churches today than Spirit-filled incendiary fellowships that help people explode with more love, more compassion, more joy, more holiness, more zeal for God, more boldness in witness, more power in ministry. Andrew Murray, in his day, lamented the sad state of the church of Christ on earth. Just think, he said, of the "hundreds and thousands of honest, earnest Christians who are not living a life in the power of God or to His glory. So little power, so little devotion or consecration to God, so little perception of the truth that a Christian is to be utterly surrendered to God's will!"[12] Fellowship is a God-given way to surrender to God, connect to life in the power of the Spirit, and enter into partnership with God in reaching a broken and lost world.

Entering In

Are you ready for a fresh vision of the explosive possibilities of Christian fellowship? May we all commit to being a part of ordinary Christians meeting in houses and groups in our neighborhoods, spurring one another on toward love and good deeds, asking God with expectancy and fervency that the Spirit would be poured out, that people would be added to our fellowships weekly, that our witness would be bold, that prison doors would be opened, and that we be united in love with a common mind and purpose.

Right now:

Take a few minutes to reflect on the fellowship God has already given to you. Ask "Who knows me? With whom can I be honest and vulnerable? Who loves me enough to be honest with me?" Thank God for these friends and ask him to deepen your partnership with them. Pray:

Lord, I know that without fellowship I am captive to the individualism of my culture and lost in self-preoccupation. I need you, working through others, to be growing me into your likeness. May all the gifts and possibilities you have created in me be released for your glory and the benefit of others. In Jesus' name, Amen.

In the coming days and weeks:

❧ Remember that gathering together with fellow believers connects you with the power of the Holy Spirit. Join a small group or begin a small group in your home that can be a place for sharing, worship, prayer, support, challenge, and ministry.

✢ Gather two or three friends into a weekly accountability group for spiritual growth. Ask one another: "How has God spoken to you through the Scripture this week. What has been your experience in prayer and meditation. What temptations have you faced? Do you have any sins to confess? What occasions have you seized to serve others?" Then pray for one another, confessing sins, receiving forgiveness, giving encouragement, and spurring one another on toward love and good deeds.

✢ Make an effort this week to tear down any walls of hostility between you and others (see Eph. 2:11–22). Let Christ be the mediator as you make peace with others in your community of faith.

✢ Is there someone the Holy Spirit wants to draw into fellowship through you? Someone who needs support, encouragement, accountability, or challenge? Make plans to reach out to that person or family through prayer, a phone call, a letter, an invitation to dinner, or some shared event.

✢ Seeking the good of others, speaking truthfully to your neighbor, being rid of all bitterness, being kind and compassionate, having patience, loving one another, carrying one another's burdens—these are a few examples from Scripture of how we can demonstrate the love of God in the midst of our communities of faith. For the next month, put one or two of these actions into practice each week as a demonstration of your desire for and commitment to Christian fellowship.

12

Simplicity

———•———

"G od made human beings straightforward," says the author of Ecclesiastes, "but they have devised many schemes" (Ecc. 7:29 NRSV). We have been made to be upright and simple, to be in love and harmony with God, but we complicate our lives through lustful schemes that put us into bondage to greed and materialism. Through the spiritual discipline of simplicity we are able to move against the desires of our flesh and the swift stream of our culture toward a life of single-mindedness and unity with God. As George McDonald noted: "To have what we want is riches, but to be able to do without is power."

We live in a complex world. Our schedules are hectic, our lifestyles frantic. Enormous amounts of information are thrown at us through every conceivable means. Advertisements shout at us, trying to convince us that "more" or "newer" or "bigger" is better. Our culture entices us to work more so that we can gain more so that we can buy more. Yet the things we buy do not satisfy us. Instead we feel more exhausted, drained, frustrated, and empty inside than ever before. In the midst of all this mad rush and insane complexity, God calls us to what is best for us—simplicity of lifestyle.

Simplicity is practicing a lifestyle free of excess, greed, and covetousness so that we can draw closer to God and reach out to others in compassionate service. As we enter into simplicity, the Holy Spirit empowers us to seek first the kingdom of God, to keep our eyes on Jesus, and to live free of crippling anxiety and lust for money.

The Bible gives us clear and unambiguous teaching about the dangers of accumulation: "You shall not covet" (Ex. 20:17); "Though your riches increase, do not set your heart on them" (Ps. 62:10); "Whoever trusts in his riches will fall" (Prov. 11:28); "Be on your guard against all kinds of greed; a man's life does not consist in the abundance of his possessions" (Luke 12:15); "People who want to get rich fall into temptation and a trap and into many foolish and harmful desires that plunge men into ruin and destruction. For the love of money is a root of all kinds of evil" (1 Tim. 6:9–10).

Jesus commanded that we should not store up treasure for ourselves here on earth because where our treasure is, there will our hearts be (Matt. 6:19–21). He knew our human propensity to worship and serve the very thing that gains our focus, so he charged us to "seek first his kingdom and his righteousness" (Matt. 6:33). To possess the kingdom we must be like the man who joyfully sold all he had in order to secure the hidden treasure he found in a field; we must be like the pearl merchant who sold all he had in order to possess one pearl of great price. The kingdom of God is ours when everything else takes second place.

Siang-Yang grew up in a culture that prized degrees, titles, and honors. Over the years he has had to learn to turn away from these cultural "rewards" and not let them define his worth. When he has been tempted to the contrary, the Holy Spirit reminds him of his mother, who still lives in Singapore. She is humble and unassuming. She is not much impressed with honors and titles. She never had an opportunity to go to school and cannot read or write Chinese or English. Yet she is among the most simple, caring, and loving people he knows.

Siang-Yang wants his heart and his life to be more like that of his mother. Our hearts and character are of far greater importance to God than external degrees, honors, or titles. Jesus warned that we are not to justify ourselves before others. God alone knows our hearts: "What is highly valued among men is detestable in God's sight" (Luke 16:15).

Simplicity opens us to the transforming work of the Holy Spirit. It is a practical and concrete way of losing our lives for

Christ's sake and the gospel—counting everything we have as loss for the sake of knowing him. If we take Jesus seriously, we must acknowledge him to be Lord of all the areas of our lives. We must surrender all our relationships, resources, careers, and futures to his lordship. We are to seek him and his kingdom first in all that we do. A sure sign of our desire to follow Jesus is a lifestyle of growing simplicity.

The Work of the Holy Spirit in Simplicity

In order to live simply we need the power of the Holy Spirit. The early disciples lived simply, sharing all they had with each other out of loving generosity and genuine compassion, because of the power of the Spirit that had come upon them (see Acts 2, 4). They were so filled with the Holy Spirit, so in love with God, so united in faith and love for one another, so ready to believe, to obey, to give, to suffer, and, if need be, to die, that their acts of generosity, hospitality, and mercy were the most natural and obvious actions to undertake.[1] These early fellowships had been taken over by the Holy Spirit and transformed in every aspect of their life together.

As we grow in simplicity the Holy Spirit produces fruit in our lives that includes greater love and self-control. This love and self-control help us break our enslavement to greed, covetousness, and other lusts of the flesh. The Holy Spirit also releases spiritual gifts in us—such as giving, mercy, hospitality, and voluntary poverty—that free us to serve and reach out to others.

All Christians are supposed to give, but for those with the spiritual gift of giving (Rom. 12:8) it is quite natural, in response to the Spirit's leading, to give generously and cheerfully of their money and other material possessions such as clothes, cars, and property.[2] In so doing they are entering more deeply into the discipline of simplicity.

To live by the Spirit through the spiritual gift of mercy also leads one more deeply into simplicity. Those with the spiritual gift of mercy (Rom. 12:8) feel genuine empathy and compassion for individuals who suffer physical, mental, or emotional problems, and translate that compassion into deeds of mercy that reflect Christ's love. This can be as simple as bringing food to an elderly neighbor who is sick and living alone, or baby-sitting for a young couple who desperately need some time away for a weekend. Or it can be as involving as volunteering several hours each week in a center that provides food and shelter for the homeless.

The spiritual gift of hospitality is a beautiful outward expression of simplicity. Those with the spiritual gift of hospitality (1 Peter 4:9) are drawn by the Holy Spirit to open their homes to those in need of food and lodging. They find it rewarding to regularly make room in their lives for a hurting person who needs consistent love and a stable family environment. The Holy Spirit helps to create heart-to-heart bonds of love and affection between people so that the person with this gift is supernaturally enabled to welcome others, including people they may not know well or at all!

Still other individuals are empowered by the Holy Spirit to enter into voluntary poverty (1 Cor. 13:1–3), adopting the lifestyle of those living at the poverty level in a given society in order to love and serve them more effectively. Those who have this gift count it all joy to renounce material possessions and luxury for the sake of ministering to others in service to God. Mother Teresa and her Sisters all over the world live in the simplicity of voluntary poverty as part of their commitment to witness the love of God to the poorest of the poor.

A word of caution: It is a mistake to idealize poverty or to think that riches are innately wrong. Living simply for most of us means being good stewards of the financial resources God has given to us. Stewardship, which requires possessions and anticipates giving, walks the path of simplicity between idealized poverty and isolating wealth. True simplicity reorients our lives so that our possessions, instead of possessing and destroying us, can be enjoyed, shared, and freely given to others in need.

A lifestyle of simplicity, without the Holy Spirit, can be just another anxiety-laden attempt to please God or impress others. Until we experience God's gracious power and provision flowing to us, we are not free to let it flow through us to others. Generous giving, warm hospitality, acts of mercy, and identification with the poor can all be dry and artificial attempts at self-justification rather than acts of love and service in response to a loving and giving God. We need to follow the lead of the disciples, who learned through experience that their first priority was to seek the kingdom first, and once they entered into its life and power that they were liberated to serve one another in unprecedented ways.[3]

The Spirit works through the spiritual discipline of simplicity to keep our focus on God and his kingdom, helping us to reach out in love and service to others. As he leads us into simplicity, he will bring our character and lifestyle into a simple, single-minded obedience to God's will and conformity to the image of Christ.

Contentment in Simplicity

Simplicity is an invitation into true contentment. "Keep your lives free from the love of money and be content with what you have," says the author of Hebrews (Heb. 13:5). Paul learned the secret of being content no matter what his circumstances. In every situation, whether he had little or much, whether he was well fed or hungry, he knew he could get through anything by the strength of the Lord (Phil. 4:11–13). Participants in the early church learned such contentment as well: no matter what their circumstances—persecution, famine, or sword—they were free to care for others with compassion. They knew that nothing could separate them from the love of God.

The history of the church is replete with examples of men and women who knew contentment in simplicity. In the thirteenth century, Francis of Assisi pursued simplicity with a passion. He felt blessed in having nothing, because he was free to enjoy everything. Unimpressed by numbers, success, rank, or degrees, he chose vulnerability instead of security, truth instead of practicality, honesty instead of influence. He turned the values of his day upside down, not because this was fashionable, but because it seemed to him to be common sense. He discovered the pearl of great price—the kingdom of God and God himself—the possession of which all other things were worth abandoning, and he held to this course till the end of his life.

Francis called those who followed after him "friars minor," which means little, unimportant ones. He wanted his followers to mingle with the world without becoming entangled with the world. He taught them to see things simply, to be gentle and forgiving toward all people. Humility and simplicity were a natural consequence of hearts overflowing with love and worship of God. Francis knew that if his friars had many possessions, they would begin to focus on ways to protect them. In contrast, having nothing, his friars could go anywhere, even among the rich or powerful, because there was nothing to hold them. Nothing could hold them because they had hold of nothing. G. K. Chesterton said of Francis and his friars:

> You could not threaten to starve a man who was ever striving to fast. You could not ruin him and reduce him to beggary, for he was already a beggar. There was a very lukewarm satisfaction even in beating him with a stick, when he only indulged in little leaps and cries of joy because indignity was his only dignity. You could not put his head in a halter without risk of putting it in a halo.[4]

Hudson Taylor, founder of the China Inland Mission in the nineteenth century, was greatly strengthened in his call to service by the practice of simplicity, in which he experienced great joy and blessing. He said:

> I believe we are all in danger of accumulating—it may be from thoughtlessness, or from pressure of occupation—things which would be useful to others, while not needed by ourselves, and the retention of which entails loss of blessing. If the whole resources of the Church of God were well utilized, how much more might be accomplished! How many poor might be fed, and naked clothed, and to how many of those as yet unreached the Gospel might be carried![5]

Years ago, Doug collected old coins as a hobby. When he was feeling really good about things, or when he was especially discouraged or depressed, he would go shopping and buy a few coins. He did not realize how dependent he had become on this pattern, and others like it, to give meaning and purpose to his life until he was more fully in love with and surrendered to Jesus.

One day Doug realized he hadn't bought a coin for nearly a year, and it dawned on him that he no longer needed to buy things to be content. Having found the pearl of great price, he was free to let go of all other things. It was great fun and a wonderful blessing for Doug to begin giving his coins away and to understand that all his possessions really belonged to God. He has been slowly learning ever since to let the Spirit guide him in giving away or sharing with others the things God has entrusted to him.

The heroes of our modern culture are those who are instantly rich—the plumber who wins twenty-four million dollars in the New York lottery, the sports star who signs with a new team for five million dollars a year. Wealth has become an idol. Lost in the shadows is the ideal of the rich boy who voluntarily becomes poor. We have wonderful images and pictures of heroes in the Christian tradition, but do we celebrate them? Do we put them forth to challenge the current cultural idolatries? Do we understand that St. Francis danced all the time in the midst of poverty because in the midst of his poverty he had nothing but Jesus, and he had so much joy he could not contain himself? Do we realize that in our crazy upside-down culture, covetousness is now called ambition, hoarding is called prudence, and greed is called industry?[6]

We won't be content until we enter into the practice of simplicity. It is what we are made for. Jesus will become real and the Father's love will become tangible when the world sees among Christians a simple, Spirit-empowered lifestyle of radical, loving service.

Generosity

If it is in giving that we receive, then we should be eager to be generous in our giving. Generosity emanates from the heart of

God. The apostle Paul reminds us of how much the Lord gave for our sakes, as he went to the cross to save us: "For you know the grace of our Lord Jesus Christ, that though he was rich, yet for your sakes he became poor, so that you through his poverty might become rich" (2 Cor. 8:9). God wants us to be generous people, giving cheerfully, in deep gratitude for what he has given us (see 2 Cor. 9:6–15). Since "the earth is the LORD'S, and everything in it" (Ps. 24:1), the Lord is the true owner of our money, wealth, and possessions. We are only stewards of what he has given to us. The right question to be asking then is not "How much should I give away?" but "How much of God's money is it good for me to keep?"

Hudson Taylor learned the joy of proportionate giving. In order to prepare for the hardships he expected to encounter in the mission field, he determined to get along on as little as possible:

> I soon found that I could live upon very much less than I had previously thought possible. Butter, milk, and other such luxuries I soon ceased to use; and I found that by living mainly on oatmeal and rice, with occasional variations, a very small sum was sufficient for my needs. In this way I had more than two-thirds of my income available for other purposes; and my experience was that the less I spent on myself and the more I gave away, the fuller of happiness and blessing did my soul become. Unspeakable joy all the day long, and every day, was my happy experience. God ... was a living, bright reality, and all I had to do was joyful service.[7]

Jesus dealt with possessions in such a radical way because he knew our possessions too often possess us. We are acquisitive by nature; we have to be taught to share. Owning and possessing, not giving, are natural to our unconverted selves. "Owning" is the most obvious trait of sinful human nature, "mine" is its favorite adjective, and "keep" is its most cherished verb. In contrast, Evelyn Underhill once said that the saints she knew in the flesh seemed quite unable to keep anything for themselves.[8]

Generosity begins with the giving of ourselves. Paul wrote to the Corinthians about the generosity of the Macedonian churches and about how they first gave themselves to the Lord (2 Cor. 8:2–5). This is the heartbeat of generosity. Once we belong to God, once we experience his love and goodness, then we will naturally experience generosity as we give to others in keeping with God's will.

Paul reveals a wonderful pattern of giving in his description of the Macedonian's generosity.[9] First, they gave *gladly*, with overflowing joy, in the midst of their poverty. Is this possible? Joy and poverty together? Is it possible that joyful giving comes only when we give sacrificially and not out of our abundance?

Second, the Macedonians also gave *fully*, with rich generosity. The church in Macedonia was as poor as the church in Jerusalem for whom Paul was collecting an offering. But this was no hindrance to a people whose joyful hearts created in them a desire to give even beyond their ability.

Third, they gave *freely*, entirely on their own. There is no sense of duty or legalism here, no attempt to win friends or influence people. They pleaded with Paul for the privilege of sharing in the service he was undertaking. They knew that helping to bring relief to the church in Jerusalem would release joy, meaning, and blessing for themselves.

Finally, they gave *anonymously*. No single individual or church is mentioned. The source of giving is simply the Christians from Macedonia. While it is not wrong to be known for our giving, when a gift is given anonymously we can be assured that our motivation for giving is genuine generosity, rather than to gain credit for ourselves.

Ask yourself regularly: "What is the pattern and meaning of my current practice of giving? What is the largest gift I have given recently? What were my motives for giving? Was the gift given joyfully, freely, anonymously? Was it given from my abundance, or did it require personal sacrifice and deeper trust in God that he would provide in the midst of my own need?

Everyday Simplicity

The lust for owning, gaining, and possessing has become so great in our culture that living simply requires careful thought and persistent practice. Here are some basic guidelines we have found helpful in practicing everyday simplicity.

Buy Things to Meet Your Basic Needs

This is not as easy as it sounds because the mass media hound us daily to buy the right brand names, most fashionable clothes and cars, and the latest convenience gadgets.

Ten years ago Doug's daughter Sarah, fifteen years old and looking forward to the time she would drive, began hounding Doug to sell the family's old beat-up '73 Ford Pinto station wagon. She was ashamed of the old car and would have Doug drop her off a block from her school so none of her friends would see her in the car. "I will never drive that car!" she said. Doug responded, "Sarah, if you want to drive, that is the car you will drive." Fortunately, Sarah's desire to drive turned out to be greater than her need to be in a new fancy car, but the whole experience reminded Doug how much the mass media pressure us—and especially our children—to stay in step with fashion.

Siang-Yang has learned over the years to avoid brand names and designer labels (highest cost), to buy what is useful and long-lasting (overall lower cost), to buy needed things when they are on sale (lowest cost), to not buy things he can easily share with friends or relatives (no cost), and then to give some of the money he saves to organizations that support hungry and homeless people.

Turn Away from Things That Have a Hold on You

It's great training in simplicity to regularly give things away, such as a bicycle, clothes, or a piece of equipment that you haven't used recently—even money, when you are aware of a need. Such regular giving will keep you free of possessiveness.

Think of something you value, and then imagine giving it away. Could you live without it? Do you possess it or does it possess you? Would it be good for you to be free of it? If so, give it away. By such actions we demonstrate our eagerness for the kingdom of God (see Mark 10:17–31).

A student at Fuller wrote the following in response to Psalm 73:25:

> I must admit that I often find myself desiring other things besides God: material goods, emotional strokes, human relationships, etc. Pausing to reflect, I realize that if I were to . . . release things in my life, one by one, there would come that moment when I would have only God left to me. More importantly, and more accurately, he would have me.[10]

Focus on Enjoying the Things Available That You Do Not Own

Experiencing life by availing yourself to the things and people around you, rather than focusing on your possessions can be very rewarding. These can be things such as a deepened relationship, a public park or beach, a library, or a walk in the woods. Be thankful for the things your friends and neighbors are willing to share with you, things you can enjoy and benefit from without having to buy and own. Think about ways you can share what you have with others in order to free them from having to buy or own things they only occasionally need. Deeper Christian fellowship can be experienced through such mutual caring and sharing!

Let Your Thoughts, Speech, and Actions Be Simple and Straightforward

Jesus said, "Simply let your 'Yes' be 'Yes,' and your 'No,' 'No'; anything beyond this comes from the evil one" (Matt. 5:37). A recent textbook attempt at defining love went like this: "Love . . . is the cognitive-affective state characterized by intrusive and obsessive fantasizing concerning reciprocity of amorant feeling by the object of the amorance." Imagine squeezing that onto a valentine. Better yet, imagine your loved one's response to such a message! Simplicity and clarity of thought and speech proceed from the heart. "Out of the overflow of the heart the mouth speaks," said Jesus (Matt. 12:34).[11] Keeping your speech and actions simple keeps you rooted in the basics of loving the Lord your God with all your heart, soul, mind, and strength, and your neighbor as yourself.

Look for the Holy Spirit to Be at Work When You Experience Interruptions

Often, the interruptions in life turn out to be Spirit-directed ministry opportunities, invitations from God to join him in partnership. As you live more simply, you will be more available to the Holy Spirit, and he will create opportunities for you to share your time, talent, and treasures to bless others.

Sharing with others out of your abundance or your scarcity is the heartbeat of hospitality. Set an extra place at your meal table as a reminder to be regularly asking visitors, friends, and an occasional stranger into your home for dinner. Prepare a place in your home for a stranger or sojourner the Lord may bring to you to stay for a few nights or a few weeks. Ministering in this way is ministering to the Lord. Your life will be enriched by your generosity, hospitality, and vulnerability. (You must be wise in your hospitality, discerning the Spirit's leading, so that you are not putting yourself or your family in danger from a potentially violent person.)

Turn Away from Anything That Seeks to Replace God as Your First Love

Job, ambition, family, friends, investments, property, titles, degrees, honors, hobbies, and other pursuits can so easily take control and keep us from seeking God's Kingdom first and yielding to the Lordship of Christ. Our first priority is to love the Lord our God, to serve him only, and to allow the Holy Spirit to take full control of our lives.

In living simply and giving generously, we demonstrate the reality of God's ownership of everything that we have, exhibit faith in his provision for our own needs, and show love for others and genuine concern for their needs. We become aware of how lives can be touched and blessed, including our own, as we give and share generously and gladly in thanksgiving to God (2 Cor. 9:12).

The great challenge before us is to put kingdom values into practice in our daily lives—to be simple and upright, and to move against the swift streams of our culture toward a life of single-mindedness, simplicity, and unity with God.

Entering In

Jesus challenges us to seek first God's kingdom and his right-eousness. He promises that as a result, all the things we need in life—food, drink, clothing, shelter—will be given to us as well (Matt. 6:33). Let us respond by yielding our lives and possessions more fully to the Spirit's control, receiving from him the grace to live in greater simplicity day by day.

Right now:

Read Matthew 6:19–34 and meditate on Matthew 6:33: "Seek first his kingdom and his righteousness, and all these things will be given to you as well." Pray:

Holy Spirit of God, help me to seek your kingdom first. Take control of my desires, passions, and material possessions. Help me to be a good steward of what you've given me and a generous giver from the bounty you pour down upon me. May I, in your power, live in greater simplicity, so that others may be touched and transformed by the love of Christ. In Jesus' name, Amen.

In the coming days and weeks:

❧ Take some time today to reflect on your life. In what ways are you rich? What is the extent of your wealth and pos-sessions? Do you have enough, too much? Honestly ask, "What controls me. What do I 'serve' the most? What can I give up or give away?" Ask the Holy Spirit for power to be delivered from any bondage to your possessions and expect him to show you the way into new freedom. Then, be obedient to what he tells you.

✸ Take a week to explore the area of giving. Where are you now in your practice of giving? What are your next steps into the joy of giving? If you do not already tithe, explore tithing for a month and see what happens to your heart and spirit. Look for ways to curb any unnecessary spending. Ask God how much of your money you should keep.

✸ Review the basic guidelines of everyday simplicity—buy only to meet basic needs, give away what has a hold on you, focus on enjoying what you cannot own, let thoughts and speech be simple and honest, look for God in the "interruptions," and so on. Each week during this month, put one of these ideas into practice.

✸ Spend an afternoon or weekend in a ministry center that serves wounded, sick, hungry, or homeless people. Look carefully into the faces of those you meet. Listen to their voices. Consider that these people are made in God's image, just as you are. Ask God to give you his point of view about and his heart of compassion for these people.

✸ Unclutter your life—de-accumulate. Put on a yard sale. Give away the money you gain and give away what you can't sell. Clean out your closet and give away any clothes you haven't worn for a year.

✸ Simplify your life. Give up TV for a while. Stop working so much at the office. Give up your plans to build "bigger barns" (see Luke 12:13–21). Take some long walks and talk to God about the real meaning of your life. If you release things in your life to God one by one, the day will come when he will be all you will have left. And more important, he will have you!

13

Service

———— ·◆· ————

Service is the most distinctive quality of Jesus' lifestyle and ministry. "Whoever wants to become great among you must be your servant. . . . the Son of Man did not come to be served, but to serve" (Matt. 20:26–28). Jesus calls his followers to serve one another in this same manner. Through the discipline of service, we become servants after the style of Jesus.

Ponder again Paul's description of Jesus as the one who humbled himself, "taking the very nature of a servant," and becoming obedient unto death (Phil. 2:7–8). This should be our attitude, says Paul. Why? Because this is the heart, mind, and attitude of Jesus; it is the lifestyle that God blesses and raises up; it is what God intended in creating us. As E. Stanley Jones said, "We are structured for the outgoingness of the love of the Kingdom. It is our native land."[1] We are God's "currency," to be spent by him to bless, heal, and restore others. Through the spiritual discipline of service, we are involved in a great adventure with the Holy Spirit, following his lead into loving service and sacrifice for the sake of Christ and the Kingdom.

Service flows naturally out of a love relationship with God. For example, it is in our worship (see chapter 10) that we are given fresh motivation for mission and ministry. Following his vision of God's holiness, Isaiah said, "Here I am, send me." Worship leads to empowered service. A. W. Tozer wrote: "No one can long worship God in spirit and in truth before the obligation to holy service becomes too strong to resist. . . . Fellowship with God leads straight to obedience and good works. That is the divine order and it can never be reversed."[2]

Service, then, is our natural response of "holy obedience" that flows from our passion for God. As we enter into the discipline of service, we gain the mind of Christ and grow in openness to God. We become more sensitive to God's presence, more discerning of God's will, and more submissive to the Spirit's work. Service is a concrete expression of our love for Jesus and our desire to be more like him.

Gifted by the Holy Spirit for Service

All Christians are gifted by the Holy Spirit for various kinds of service. First Peter 4:10 says, "Each one should use whatever gift he has received to serve others, faithfully administering God's grace in its various forms." If you are a Christian, you have spiritual gifts! Further, God's purpose in giving you spiritual gifts is for you to serve with them for the building up of his kingdom. "To each one of us grace has been given," says Paul, to be apostles, prophets, evangelists, pastors, and teachers, "to prepare God's people for works of service, so that the body of Christ may be built up until we all reach unity in the faith and in the knowledge of the Son of God and become mature, attaining to the whole measure of the fullness of Christ" (Eph. 4:7, 11–13).

The power of the Holy Spirit is released as we exercise the gifts of the Spirit in works of service for the building up of the body. Whether we serve in exhorting, teaching, giving, prayers for healing, or acts of mercy, we are dependent on the power and guidance of the Holy Spirit for effective spiritual contribution to the whole body of Christ.

At the moment of conversion, when we say yes to Jesus and accept his lordship, the Holy Spirit comes to live in us, bringing spiritual gifts which he distributes according to his sovereign will. "There are different kinds of gifts, but the same Spirit.... All these are the work of one and the same Spirit, and he gives them to each one, just as he determines" (1 Cor. 12:4, 11).

Paul also says there are "varieties of service" (1 Cor. 12:5 NRSV). *Diakoniai*, the Greek word for service, suggests an eager readiness to serve. So gifts are evident in the lives of those eager to serve and willing to be used by God. While the Holy Spirit gives spiritual gifts to each person as he wills, we are still encouraged to earnestly desire and seek the spiritual gifts (1 Cor. 12:31, 14:1).

In the process of eagerly seeking and willingly receiving spiritual gifts, we face several difficulties. Sometimes, when we seek after spiritual gifts without seeming to receive them, we become discouraged and disillusioned. We must trust that the Holy Spirit knows us better than we know ourselves and sees when we are ready to receive and rightly motivated to use his gifts. The right motivation for all Spirit-filled service is to give glory to God (1 Peter 4:11).

At other times, in seeking gifts, we can think we receive and yet be deceived. In our eagerness to serve others through our spiritual gifts, we can be involved in something only partially of God, or even something counterfeit. And when our seeking for gifts is rewarded, and new and rich avenues for service and ministry are opened up to us, we face the danger of spiritual pride.

It takes time to grow into healthy and well-balanced ministry. All of us will experience times of discouragement along the way as we eagerly request, explore, and exercise gifts of the Spirit. We will sometimes be wrong, or misguided, in using spiritual gifts, but the balance and correction the Spirit provides through Scripture and Christian fellowship will help us to mature. The Holy Spirit teaches us as much through our mistakes as through our successes. And in the process, we will experience the joy, excitement, and gratitude that come through partnership with the Holy Spirit in Spirit-filled service.

As we earnestly seek what the Holy Spirit gives only according to his sovereign will, our patient and persistent requests will, over time, bring us into God's will. Time is on God's side—time for the Holy Spirit to shape our character, refine our motives, and get us ready to receive in healthy ways.

How do we know what gifts the Spirit has for us and how God wants us to serve? As Paul advises, we are to think about ourselves "with sober judgment, in accordance with the measure of faith God has given," because we all "have different gifts, according to the grace given us" (Rom. 12:3, 6). That means we are to have a realistic estimate of our abilities in the context of the faith and grace God has given to us. Peter Wagner suggests five simple guidelines to help you discover what gifts the Spirit has for you and which areas God might want to use you in service.[3]

1. Explore the possibilities. Study the Scripture (1 Cor. 12; Rom. 12; Eph. 4; 1 Peter 4), read books about the gifts of the Spirit,[4] and talk to people who you believe are gifted in areas you want to explore. When you resonate with someone else's gifts, it may be the Spirit's way of helping you to identify your own gifts.

2. Begin to experiment with the gifts you feel drawn to. Allow time for the Spirit to confirm and develop the gifts he has for you. The Holy Spirit will present you with needs and opportunities. As you respond, you will find out where you are useful and how you are drawn to serve. Keep a dialogue going with God about what he is doing and how he wants you to serve.

3. Examine your motivation and feelings. When you enjoy doing something, you usually do a better job at it. The Holy Spirit will generally match spiritual gifts with your temperament, abilities, personality, and experience so that you will say, "This is what I really enjoy doing; I'd rather be doing this than anything else!" The Scripture promises that if you "Delight yourself in the LORD ... he will give you the desires of your heart" (Ps. 37:4).

4. Evaluate your effectiveness. What is God accomplishing through you? Where are you effective in helping people. Where are you getting positive feedback? If you have the gift of healing, people should be getting well. If you have the gift of teaching, people should be edified. When you

operate in the gifts of the Holy Spirit, there will be good results.

5. Expect confirmation of your gift(s) to come from the body of Christ. Don't rely on just your feelings, wishes, or dreams. What God has given you will be confirmed in many ways, but especially by others in the faith.

As we serve others through spiritual gifts, we are to "do it with the strength God provides, so that in all things God may be praised through Jesus Christ. To him be the glory and the power for ever and ever. Amen" (1 Peter 4:11).

In the Style of Jesus

Jesus lived out a lifestyle of servanthood and called his disciples to do the same. He sent them out to "preach ... , heal the sick, cleanse the lepers, raise the dead, cast out demons" (Matt. 10:7–8 NRSV). When he called Peter and Andrew to follow after him, it was to become "fishers of men," bearers of the good news to others (Mark 1:17). They were to be messengers of peace, healing the sick and saying "the kingdom of God is near you" (Luke 10:9).

The disciples were tempted by ambition, arguing among themselves about who was greatest. They desired status instead of service. Jesus told the disciples: "Whoever wants to become great among you must be your servant" (Matt. 20:26). When we become servants of others, we are moving toward God as he really is—a God who has won the right to rule us because he came in the flesh to serve us. God wants to be known to us through servanthood.[5] Our service will be natural and Spirit-filled when we are ambitious for God's kingdom alone, serving others with the loving, gracious, and humble spirit of our servant, Jesus.

Jesus demonstrated this spirit of service to his disciples in an unforgettable way by wrapping a towel around his waist, kneeling down before them, washing their feet, and drying them with the towel that was wrapped around him (John 13:3–17). Peter was horrified at this action; it did not fit his notions of Jesus' royalty.

The act of washing the feet of a tired traveler was so humble that even Jewish slaves were not expected to perform this most menial act of service.

"You shall never wash my feet," Peter declared. To which Jesus replied, "Unless I wash you, you have no part with me" (John 13:8). Jesus was helping Peter understand that Christians meet God at the place of service. We meet God as a foot washer or we do not meet him at all. The towel becomes the mark of those who have let the King serve them, the symbol that distinguishes those who know and follow the Servant-King.[6]

After washing and drying their feet with the towel, Jesus told his disciples to listen carefully to what he had to say: "Now that I, your Lord and Teacher, have washed your feet, you also should wash one another's feet. I have set you an example that you should do as I have done for you.... Now that you know these things, you will be blessed if you do them" (v. 14–15, 17).

We cannot be servants without personal involvement. We are to act with Christlike unselfishness that goes against the grain of our pride and desire for control. We are to be obedient in our service. Servants in the style of Jesus will not escape pain and suffering, but they will have the ultimate joy of knowing Christ's presence.[7] Paul says, "We are hard pressed on every side, but not crushed; perplexed, but not in despair; persecuted, but not abandoned; struck down, but not destroyed" (2 Cor. 4:8–9). We are servants for Jesus' sake, and the power to be servants comes from God (vv. 5–7).

Jesus lived a compassionate life and calls us to be people of compassion—which means "to suffer with."

> Compassion asks us to go where it hurts, to enter into places of pain, to share in brokenness, fear, confusion, and anguish. Compassion challenges us to cry out with those in misery, to mourn with those who are lonely, to weep with those in tears. Compassion requires us to be weak with the weak, vulnerable with the vulnerable, and powerless with the powerless. Compassion means full immersion in the condition of being human.[8]

Jesus' disciples felt called to make God's compassion present in this world by moving with Jesus into positions of servanthood. Peter urged his readers to put on humility and be servants of one another (1 Peter 5:5). They heard Jesus say that the one who is humble will be exalted; the one who surrenders life for his sake and the gospel will receive life; the one who becomes as a little child will be the greatest in the kingdom of heaven (Luke 14:11, Mark 8:35, Matt. 18:4).

This frightens us at first. Who wants to be humble? Who wants to surrender? Who wants to be like a small, powerless child? All this runs against the grain of our natural inclinations. But when we understand that this pathway allows us to participate in the ongoing self-revelation of God, we can joyfully choose it as the pathway into his loving heart. For those who want to proclaim God's presence in the world, servanthood becomes the most natural response.[9]

Motivation for Service

In our flesh we resist the call to be servants in the style of Jesus. We want to serve, but we want to choose whom we will serve and the circumstances of our service. We prefer to serve in ways that keep us in control and that bring recognition to ourselves. Maxie Dunham writes:

> The way most of us serve keeps us in control. We choose whom, when, where, and how we will serve. We stay in charge. Jesus is calling for something else. He is calling us to be servants. When we make this choice, we give up the right to be in charge. The amazing thing is that when we make this choice we experience great freedom. We become available and vulnerable, and we lose our fear of being stepped on, or manipulated, or taken advantage of. Are not these our basic fears? We do not want to be in a position of weakness.[10]

In controlling our service we run the risk of spiritual pride. We become vulnerable to a "good works" mentality, where we think we are pleasing God or impressing others through our service. We become angry when those we are serving aren't appropriately grateful. We become self-righteous in our service. By the power of the Holy Spirit, we must reject self-righteous service as a sinful motivation and take upon ourselves the humble spirit of Jesus, counting others better than ourselves (Phil. 2:3, Rom. 12:3). Can we serve our coworkers by helping them to succeed, and then be joyful when they are promoted and affirmed? Can we put aside our fears of being neglected and humbly serve those God has raised to positions of importance, trusting God to lift us up at the proper time? Can we pray and work for the ministry of others to prosper when it might mean that our ministry is overshadowed?[11]

Rees Howells, a central figure in the Welsh revivals of the early twentieth century, was challenged by the Holy Spirit to surrender leadership in the mission he had started, to come along behind the new leader to intercede for him, and to pray that the ministry would be even more successful in his hands. Rees had put all his time and money into the mission for three years and it was a great inward conflict for him to allow someone else to get the credit. As he responded obediently to the Spirit's leading and entered a time of hidden service of prayer and encouragement, he discovered there was "as much joy in a hidden life of service as in an open and successful one." He was in the Spirit's training school for service, and the lessons he learned in his early ministry prepared him for deeper surrender in prayer and service for the whole of his life. He was helped during this time of surrender by the story of Madam Guyon who, even in prison, would pray, "I ask no more, in good or ill, but union with Thy holy will."[12]

Rees Howells trusted in the Holy Spirit. Can we do the same? When we stay attentive to what the Spirit is doing instead of worrying about what we are doing, our pride is checked. As we respond to God's leading, we will more likely serve genuine needs rather than our own need to serve. When our service is Spirit-filled, energy will be released for the person we are serving to be helped and healed.

We are called to be servants of Christ and to enter into service until our lives become spontaneous expressions of his servant lifestyle. Our motivation for service is love (2 Cor. 5:14–15). We are free to love because God first loved us (1 John 4:19), and our service to others is our response of love to him. We won't be at rest until we express our love for him by entering into his service.

Servant Leaders

Our human tendency is to think more highly of ourselves than we ought to, especially as we gain influence, prestige, or rank in our social, business, academic, or religious settings. As we possess more skills and responsibilities and wealth, the greater is the temptation to pride and arrogance. Jesus' call for us to be servants should cause us to reflect on our current circumstances. The higher, the more honorable, the more financially rewarded our position in life, the more it should be directed to the benefit of others and the more diligent we must be in serving and encouraging others. Service for others is the true measure of greatness (Mark 10:42–45). Our society is in distress, in desperate need of a renewed vision of servant leadership—of people shaped in the image of Jesus who understand that true life is gained in service.

Leaders who serve lead by action and example. Their time and resources are available to others. They listen and understand before acting, which builds strength and trust in followers who see the leader as a servant first. Service is aimed at the growth of those being served—are they becoming freer, more responsible; are they being empowered to become servant leaders themselves? Servant leaders are willing to lay their lives down for others, giving time, money, and energy to bring healing and reconciliation. They are motivated by a desire to be healed of the pride, distrust, and selfishness that pervade our culture. They know that true fulfillment lies in service rather than in accumulation of wealth, worldly success, or manipulation of others. It is in giving that we receive.[13]

Paul planted churches across the Mediterranean world of his day with one goal—to serve others in the name of Jesus. Paul's servant attitudes and actions gave his ministry authority and credibility among the people (see 2 Cor. 6:4–10). Paul could even celebrate his weakness because he knew that in his weakness the Holy Spirit's power would be strong (1 Cor. 2:1–5).

John Woolman, an eighteenth-century Quaker, traveled during the thirty years that preceded the Revolutionary War, up and down the Eastern Seaboard visiting Quaker families with slaves. He asked them what their ownership of slaves did to them as moral persons and what example it set for their children. In a gentle and loving way he persuaded people one by one that a wrong could be righted by individual action. His clear vision resulted in abolition of slavery as an accepted practice among the Quakers. If, in those days, there had been thirty or fifty John Woolmans, might this have prevented the Civil War a hundred years later with its six hundred thousand casualties?

Vladimir Lenin, prime architect of the Russian Revolution, said near the end of his life: "I made a mistake. Without doubt, an oppressed multitude had to be liberated. But our method only provoked further oppression and atrocious massacres. . . . It is too late now to alter the past, but what was needed to save Russia were ten Francis of Assisi's."[14]

Our service cannot change the past, but it will affect the future. In serving there is real joy, happiness, and good fruit, "multiplying thirty, sixty and a hundred times" (Mark 4:8), pouring over to bless the whole world. We can be people who make a difference, people of servant vision who can call others to responsible participation in solving injustices and inequities of our time, women and men determined to live the servant lifestyle of Jesus.

Acts of Service

Our lives are to be testing grounds for the will of God. We are to be "living sacrifices," not conformed to this world but transformed by the renewal of our minds, that we might be able "to test and approve what God's will is—his good, pleasing and perfect will" (Rom. 12:1–2). The earliest Christian communities proved the will of God in their sharing and service. They added people daily to their numbers who were drawn by the attractiveness of their loving service.

Today, the world needs to see a lifestyle among Christians of radical loving service. The kingdom vision Jesus has given us of servant leadership must be put into practice and reflected in our daily living. "By this everyone will know that you are my disciples," Jesus said, "if you have love for one another" (John 13:35 NRSV). Paul adds, "Serve one another in love" (Gal. 5:13). Love and service are the certifiable marks of discipleship to Jesus.

What would it look like for Christlike love and service to mark our lives on a daily basis? For starters, judgmentalism would have to go. We would have to be patient with each other, more compassionate, willing to go the extra mile, taking time to stand in each others' shoes, encouraging one another, praying for one another. John Calvin said praying for others is the very best way we can love them. If we prayed for others before we judged them, the Holy Spirit would filter out much of our judgment and give us his perspective on things. James gave good advice: talk less, listen more (James 1:19).

Do you find it difficult to relate to some of your coworkers or coworshipers? Pray for them and find some hidden way to serve them. This will begin to give you Christ's mind about them and free you from the tyranny of self-importance. Seventeenth-century scholar Jeremy Taylor wrote in his *Rule and Exercises of Holy Living:* "Nurture a love to do good things in secret, concealed from the eyes of others, and therefore not highly esteemed because of them. Be content to go without praise ..."[15]

Service begins with the most simple acts of respect and kindness—being on time for appointments, keeping one's commitments and promises, bringing food to a sick neighbor, sending a card of appreciation or affirmation, letting people know that you noticed their kindness or encouragement, listening—small things done with great love.

Volunteer! The things we do that we don't get paid for speak volumes about our character and allegiance to Christ. Our fellowships need the release of our gifts and energy-—as music leaders, members of the prayer ministry team, ushers, small group leaders, sponsors for the youth group, members of administrative committees and boards, and more. This is not service for the sake of self-justification, or to look good in the eyes of others. Rather, it is service as a natural response to God's love and example, service that flows from the "rest" and "easy yoke" of our relationship with Jesus (Matt. 11:28–30).

Before embarking on any service, let the Holy Spirit be your guide. Rees Howells, following his initial filling with the Holy Spirit, was told by the Spirit "that effectual praying must be guided praying, and that he was no longer to pray for all kinds of things at his own whim or fancy, but only the prayers that the Holy Spirit gave him."[16] The first prayer the Holy Spirit prayed through him was for a young man named Will Battery, an alcoholic who had been left in a weakened condition by meningitis. Battery was dirty, unshaven, wore no socks, and hadn't slept in a bed for two years. The Holy Spirit told Rees that he was to love and serve Will Battery and "pray him through to sanity and salvation."

"It wouldn't have come to my mind to love him," Rees said, "but when the Holy Ghost comes in, He brings in the love of the Saviour. It seemed as though I could lay down my life for this man; there was a love pouring out of me that I never knew before." Rees began to spend all his free time with Will, made a friend of him, and prayed for him every day. He had more joy by the Holy Spirit in seeking to win Will to Christ than being in the company of other believers. "I hadn't the faintest idea of the love of the Holy Ghost for a lost soul, until He loved one through me," he said. On Christmas day, Rees reflected,

> I had the joy of spending my first Christmas after the Holy Ghost came in, in the tin mill with this young man, from 10 a.m. to 6 p.m. My mother gave me a basket with Christmas dinner for the two of us; but my joy was too great to eat. Battery had the lot! At 4 p.m. he asked if he could come with me to the cottage meeting. What joy I had in walking with him

there! I had never asked him to go myself, for fear of embarrassing him."[17]

Howells prayed for and served Battery over the next three years until he was a thoroughly converted and transformed man. He started with the Holy Spirit, and said, "in this way I loved just one; and if you love one, you can love many; and if many, you can love all."[18]

Imagine if even one out of ten people in your circle of work set their hearts to follow after the Holy Spirit in serving others on a daily basis. Would things be different? Would the whole environment change? Would love begin to abound in a contagious tidal wave of service? Could it begin with you?

This is a great and wonderful adventure to be approached with excitement, anticipation, and joy, for God is in it. Imagine entering your workplace—or any familiar setting—silently asking, "What are you doing, Holy Spirit? What are you preparing? Who are you calling to yourself?" and then acting in response to God's leading. You may be guided by the Spirit to sit next to someone and to be open and available in conversation. The person you are sitting next to might turn out to be despondent over a failed relationship and despairing of life itself. You become the presence of God in that person's life. This is costly. You may lose control of your schedule, your time, your assurance of a good night's sleep. But what an adventure! In serving in this way, you are a living sacrifice to God. You are loving and serving the way Christ loves and serves, and he promises to bless you a hundredfold and fill you with the fullness of his joy. Christian living is *the* great adventure! E. Stanley Jones writes:

> The most miserable people in the world are the people who are self-centered, who don't do anything for anybody except themselves. They are centers of misery with no exception. . . . On the contrary, the happiest people are the people who deliberately take on themselves the sorrows and troubles of others. Their hearts sing with a strange wild joy, automatically and with no exceptions. We are struc-

tured for the outgoingness of the love of the Kingdom. It is our native land.[19]

God has called us to be servants, nothing more, nothing less. He invites us to a wedding feast. The invitation comes with an RSVP, and the response that tells him we are coming is our radical service, our availability to be shaped and empowered and used by God for his kingdom purposes.

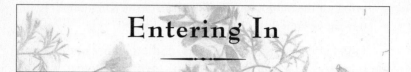

Entering In

Through the discipline of service, we become servants after the style of Jesus. He invites us all into this great, risky, vulnerable adventure of serving others in the same way that he has served us. He promises to be with us in our service to the very end. We enter into service by the power of the Holy Spirit, as his love is shed abroad in our hearts.

Right now:

Pray:

Lord, save me from the misery of self-centeredness and fit me for the outgoingness of service in your kingdom. I surrender to you today. I want to be available to be shaped and empowered and used by you for your kingdom purposes. I want to be a river of living water, a worker of signs and wonders, to reflect the brightness of Christ. Fill my heart with such love that it sings with strange and wild joy. Fill me with yourself that my life may flow in natural service to others. In your name, Servant-God, I pray. Amen.

In the days and weeks ahead:

❧ Each day this week, as you pray, ask God to bring you someone whom you can serve or give words of witness or encouragement. Determine to take action on the direction the Holy Spirit gives. Get excited! You are entering into a great adventure with the Holy Spirit.

❧ In the next week, take some time to reflect on the acts of service you have engaged in during the past few weeks. Ask yourself these questions: "Am I serving a genuine need or serving my own need to serve? In my service, am I seeking to gain control, merit, or appreciation for myself with this person or with God?" Ask God to help you to be aware of your motives and actions at the same time he is empowering you to be free as you grow in your service.

❧ Service flows naturally out of a love relationship with God. Spend time daily this week in worship to God. Let the Spirit draw you from worship into holy service and give you fresh motivation for ministry and mission. Remember the words of Tozer: "Fellowship with God leads naturally to obedience and good works."

❧ Develop a plan to earnestly desire and seek spiritual gifts to exercise in service. Review the five simple steps outlined above and begin to explore and experiment with spiritual gifts. Take time for the Holy Spirit to match spiritual gifts with your temperament, abilities, personality, and experience so that you can say, "This is what I really enjoy doing; this is how I want to serve!"

❧ "Nurture a love to do good things in secret," says Jeremy Taylor. This week let your acts of kindness go unnoticed. Pray for your coworkers. Find some hidden way to serve them. Let your faithful response to the Spirit's leading unleash a contagious tidal wave of love and service.

14

Witness

———◆———

Early this century, Sadu Sundar Singh, who was raised in the Sikh religion, was dramatically converted to Christ. Jesus came to him when Sadu Singh was desperate, saying, "Why do you persecute me? I am the Way." After this encounter, Sadu Singh, known as "the St. Paul of India," entered into a most remarkable ministry of witness. The love of Jesus flowed out of him as he moved about India proclaiming the good news of life in Jesus Christ. Like Jesus, he had no home and no possessions; he shared in the sufferings of the people he met; in the power of the Spirit, he told all who would listen of the love of God.[1]

The Holy Spirit, in filling us with the love of God, quenches the deepest thirst of our human heart. Once we have tasted living water, we want more—we are spoiled from wanting anything less. When this happens, the Spirit overflows from us to satisfy others. We are made to be witnesses to the love and goodness of God. We grow in relationship to God, receiving his love, peace, and joy, as we enter the discipline of witness.

To witness simply means to tell others, through loving actions as well as clear words, about Jesus—presenting Jesus Christ, in the power of the Holy Spirit, to people so they might receive him as Savior and serve him as Lord in the fellowship of his church.[2] The Greek verb for "evangelize" in the New Testament literally means "to share or announce good news." Witness, or evangelism, aims at bringing people into living relationship with our Father God through Jesus Christ, his only Son, by the power of the Holy Spirit.

Jesus commands us to be his witnesses—to make disciples of all nations, to be his witnesses to the ends of the earth (Matt. 28:19–20; Mark 16:15; John 20:21; Acts 1:8). But though we are commanded to be witnesses, we often have deep-seated doubts and fears about witnessing and evangelism. We hear Jesus' command to witness as a duty to perform or an action to undertake to please God instead of as a promise of blessing and an invitation to cooperate with the Holy Spirit in kingdom work. There are many reasons for this: We are afraid we will offend people with our witness. We are not sure what to say. We are afraid we won't be able to answer questions that might be asked. We may even have seen or experienced pushy and manipulative examples of witnessing and don't want to be perceived in the same way.

The primary way to overcome such fears is to fall more in love with Jesus, to give ourselves afresh to Jesus as our Lord and Savior and to develop our inner life with him by practicing the disciplines of solitude, surrender, and service. Paul Little put it well: "The beginning of spiritual reality is total commitment to Jesus Christ. . . . Inner spiritual reality developed by a secret life with God is essential for an effective witness to those who have yet to meet the God who alone can satisfy their every need."[3] Witness should not flow from a sense of obligation or guilt, but out of a heart of deep love and compassion for the lost—in tune with the heart of Jesus himself!

The Work of the Spirit in Witness

The Holy Spirit is the power behind the spiritual discipline of witness. From the moment he dwells in us he gives us the power to witness. Jesus told the disciples that when the Spirit came upon them, they would be his witnesses to the ends of the earth (Acts 1:8). This is not something that was exclusive to the disciples. Every Christian is expected to witness because every Christian is empowered to witness. The gospel we share carries with it "the power of God for the salvation of everyone who believes" (Rom. 1:16).

In the book of Acts, the relationship between the anointing of the Holy Spirit and evangelism is striking. "Go through Acts," says Martyn Lloyd-Jones, "and in every instance when we are told either that the Spirit came upon these men or that they were filled with the Spirit, you will find that it was in order to bear a witness and a testimony."[4] "Enable your servants to speak your word with great boldness," was their great concern in prayer (Acts 4:29). Acts 4:31 says, "And they were all filled with the Holy Spirit and spoke the word of God boldly." In spite of persecution, threats, and beatings, "day after day, in the temple courts and from house to house, they never stopped teaching and proclaiming the good news that Jesus is the Christ" (Acts 5:42).

The Holy Spirit had been given to the disciples not for exciting spiritual experience, not for lengthy debates about the fine points of doctrine, not to practice spiritual one-upmanship, but to give witness of Jesus Christ. As they went everywhere preaching the word, living simple and loving lives of service, sharing everything together, and testifying of their Savior, the power of the Spirit went with them.

What is filling our hearts will pour out of our mouths. If you are carrying a full glass and someone bumps you, what will spill out? Whatever is in the glass! If you are jostled and bumped in your daily life, what will "spill out" of your mouth? Whatever is filling your heart! If our hearts are full of the Spirit and filled with the love of Jesus, we are bound to witness naturally and spontaneously. The tragedy is that we often do not bear witness because we have no witness to bear. We may dutifully trot out some gospel phrases and doctrinal statements, but without the passion for Jesus and the power of the Spirit, people will not see Jesus, they will not hear Jesus, and they will not meet Jesus through us.[5] We must be filled with the Spirit to be passionate, effective witnesses.

The Spiritual Gift of Evangelist

Jesus calls and empowers all believers to be his witnesses: "You are . . . a people belonging to God, that you may declare the praises of him who called you out of darkness into his wonderful light" (1 Peter 2:9). All are to declare the praises of Jesus Christ. Though the Holy Spirit empowers *all* Christians to be witnesses for Christ, some are specifically gifted by the Holy Spirit with the spiritual gift of *evangelist* (Eph. 4:11): "the special ability that God gives to certain members of the Body of Christ to share the gospel with unbelievers in such a way that they become Jesus' disciples and responsible members of the Body of Christ."[6]

Soon after Siang-Yang was used by the Spirit to reach out to his classmates, he realized that evangelism was one of the gifts the Holy Spirit had given him—that he had a passion for the lost and a deep desire to pray for lost souls. It is common for Siang-Yang, in public settings or when traveling to speak at conferences, to pray for the Spirit's leading in helping him to be sensitive to divine appointments or opportunities to witness to others. Evangelism, for him, is one of the most exciting and joy-filled aspects of being a Christian.

Flying home from a conference recently, Siang-Yang sat next to a woman who was deeply involved in New Age and Buddhist beliefs and practices. As he began a conversation with her, she was very open and started sharing her beliefs and spiritual experiences. While listening to her, Siang-Yang prayed for the Holy Spirit to guide him and to touch this woman with the liberating truth of Christ. Here is Siang-Yang's account of what happened:

> The woman did most of the talking in our two-hour conversation. She shared about how regular meditation had helped her spiritually, and related a number of her spiritual experiences. I was able to affirm her as a deeply spiritual person who was earnestly seeking after God. I did not condemn her and her beliefs, as I might have in my earlier years, but tried to see her through the eyes of Christ, as someone made in God's image and loved deeply by Jesus. When she asked what I thought of reincarnation, I told her I didn't believe in it and proceeded to share with her how Jesus has changed my life and how unique he is.

Toward the end of our conversation, we talked about death. She was hoping that at her time of death, she would be so disciplined and focused in her mind and meditation that she would die in the right, peaceful frame of mind and would be caught up in a higher cycle of energy in the spiritual realm and then be reincarnated into a higher form of being. I shared with her that Jesus has already settled the issue of death for me, that physical death is a doorway into eternal life forever with God, and that this was true not because of my own merit or meditation or frame of mind, but solely because of what Jesus has done for all of us in his death and resurrection. We have only to accept him into our hearts to enter into his eternal embrace.

Before departing, I gave her a copy of the "Four Spiritual Laws" [published by Campus Crusade for Christ]. At her request, I gave her my business card, welcoming her to call me at any time if she wanted to talk further. . . . I have not talked to the woman since, but I know the Holy Spirit is drawing this woman to Jesus. He was at work through me to plant gospel seeds in her heart. I also know that only Jesus can satisfy the hunger of her heart!

There is a God-shaped vacuum in each of us that only God through Christ can fill. We do not need to be afraid of other religions or faiths or the New Age movement. None of them can meet the deepest needs of the human heart. Only Jesus can do that!

The religious leaders of Jesus' day looked upon the crowds and saw sinners—Gentiles, tax collectors, Samaritans—as chaff to be destroyed and burned up. But Jesus looked upon them with compassion, as a harvest to be reaped and saved. He turned to the disciples and said, "The harvest is plentiful but the workers are few. Ask the Lord of the harvest, therefore, to send out workers into his harvest field" (Matt. 9:37–38).

It is the Lord's harvest, but we are to pray for laborers and to be ready to be sent by the Spirit into the harvest to reap. Each one of us, as we've been called to Jesus, is to be a worker, a witness. Our

Lord has determined to bring in the harvest through human instruments responsive to his will.

Doing It Jesus' Way

Jesus moved constantly in the power of the Holy Spirit in his interactions with people. He didn't rush about thinking that everything depended on him or that he had to blaze the trail for God—that God was waiting on him to decide who to evangelize! Jesus kept his absolute attention on what his Father was doing. Every day Jesus asked, in effect, "Father, what are you doing today? What are you up to? You are already at work. Show me what you are doing and I will only do what I see you doing" (see John 5:17, 19–20, 30).

One day, as he was entering Jericho, Jesus observed that his Father was drawing a man named Zacchaeus to himself (Luke 19:1–10). We have no indication that Jesus had any prior knowledge of Zacchaeus. He was only doing what the Holy Spirit enables us to do in giving us a word of knowledge—moving into partnership with what God was doing. Jesus responded obediently, calling out to Zacchaeus, who was observing him from within the safe boughs of a sycamore tree. "Come down immediately," he said to Zacchaeus."I must stay at your house today." Those around Jesus were shocked at this. After all, Zacchaeus was a hated sinner and tax collector! But Zacchaeus' heart was melted by Jesus' warm acceptance. He began turning his life over to Jesus by entering into deep repentance and restitution for his sins.

Another time, passing through Samaria, Jesus encountered a woman by Jacob's well in the town of Sychar (John 4:4–42). He saw that the Father was seeking this unclean, immoral, Samaritan woman to worship him "in spirit and in truth." In obedience to his Father, and possessed of knowledge about this woman that could have come only by the Spirit, Jesus talked to her about living water (the Holy Spirit), which could become in her a spring of water welling up to eternal life. He watched her as she witnessed to her fellow Samaritans out of the overflow of her own heart, saying,

"Come, see a man who told me everything I ever did. Could this be the Christ?" God had been preparing a harvest for eternal life. Jesus' obedient response to the Spirit's leading and the passionate Spirit-directed testimony of the Samaritan woman brought forth a great reaping: "Many of the Samaritans from that town believed in him because of the woman's testimony," and as they heard him for themselves, they believed "that this man really is the Savior of the world" (v. 42).

Jesus' whole purpose was to do the will of his Father, to walk in faithful obedience to what his Father was doing. We are invited by the Spirit to walk in this same way—to "do it Jesus' way." The Scripture, church history, and the lives of contemporary faithful followers of Jesus give ample illustration of God's guidance in our work and witness, of "divine appointments" God has for his children. Paul testified that "We are God's workmanship, created in Christ Jesus to do good works, which God prepared in advance for us to do" (Eph. 2:10). The Holy Spirit arranges encounters or "appointed times" when he will give us divine guidance or release spiritual gifts in us (including gifts of faith, miracles, healing, and words of knowledge and wisdom) in order to reveal himself to an individual or group.[7]

For example, in the book of Acts, Philip was directed by God to walk along the desert road from Jerusalem to Gaza (Acts 8:26–40). As he happened by the chariot of an Ethiopian eunuch, the Holy Spirit told Philip, "Go to that chariot and stay near it" (v. 29). God had arranged a "divine appointment" for Philip in which he interpreted the Scripture to the Ethiopian, told him of the good news about Jesus, and baptized him into life in Jesus. On another occasion, Peter was guided by the Spirit to go to the house of Cornelius and give witness of Jesus. While he was speaking, "the Holy Spirit came on all who heard the message" and they were all baptized in the name of the Lord Jesus (Acts 10).

Henry Blackaby tells a story of trying to begin an outreach ministry to a nearby college campus when he was pastor at Faith Baptist Church in Saskatoon, Saskatchewan, in Canada. Following the advice of his denominational student ministries department, he tried without much success for over a year to start Bible studies in the college's resident halls. Finally he pulled the few students attending his church together and challenged them to do it Jesus' way, to go back to campus, see where God was at work, and join him.

When the students asked Blackaby how to do that, he shared two verses from Scripture the Spirit had impressed on his heart: "There is no one righteous, not even one; there is no one who understands, no one who seeks God" (Rom. 3:10–11) and "No one can come to me [Jesus] unless the Father who sent me draws him" (John 6:44). Blackaby then went on to explain that according to these passages, no one seeks God on his own or asks about spiritual things unless God is already at work. "When you see someone seeking God or asking about spiritual matters, you are seeing God at work."[8]

Blackaby sent the students back to campus with some final words of advice: "If someone starts asking you spiritual questions, whatever else you have planned, don't do it. Cancel what you are doing. Go with that individual and look to see what God is doing there." A few days later, one of the women students reported, "Oh, Pastor, a girl who has been in classes with me for two years came to me after class today. She said, 'I think you might be a Christian. I need to talk to you.' I remembered what you said. I had a class, but I missed it. We went to the cafeteria to talk. She said, 'Eleven of us girls have been studying the Bible, and none of us are Christians. Do you know somebody who can lead us in a Bible study?'"

As a result of that one contact, five Bible studies were started in the resident halls in the next few weeks. Blackaby said, "For two years we tried to do something for God and failed. For three days we looked to see where God was working and joined Him."[9] What a difference it makes when, like Jesus, we keep our eyes on God— on the work of the Holy Spirit—and do things Jesus' way.

In every situation where there is opportunity to witness, God wants us to depend on him, not on a method or strategy of evangelism. The key is not a method but a relationship. The way, the truth, and the life is a Person. We are to look to Jesus and depend on the Holy Spirit as we enter the discipline of witness.

How to Witness in the Spirit

Jesus is our best model of how to witness in the Spirit. His single-minded focus on the work of his Father enabled him to reach across social, sexual, and cultural barriers. He spoke the truth, yet his approach was humble. We can learn several things from his interaction with the woman at the well in Samaria (John 4:1–42) about how to witness in the Spirit.

Being Focused on God

Jesus determined not to do anything apart from the Father's leading. He was ready for divine appointments! In truth, he *was* a walking divine appointment for Nicodemus, Zacchaeus, Peter, Mary Magdalene, Lazarus, Mary and Martha, and countless others, including us! Jesus didn't have to go through Samaria on his journey to Galilee; in fact, most Jews took another route. He went through Samaria at the Spirit's leading because there was a divine appointment for him there with the woman at the well.[10]

Are we open to the Spirit's leading, as Jesus was? Are we willing to be available for God's purposes? Are we committed to reaching out to those around us and praying that the Holy Spirit will use us in witness? If so, we too can expect divine appointments!

Being Humble and Vulnerable

When the Samaritan woman came to draw water, Jesus asked her for a drink. This surprised the woman. Why was Jesus, a man and a Jew, asking her, a Samaritan woman, for a drink? (v. 7–9). The Holy Spirit led Jesus into a position of humility. He was tired and thirsty and did not hide his need from the woman. He modeled openness and availability through humility, thus opening the way for conversation with the woman.

Can we do the same? Can we give up control, let the social, economic, and cultural barriers come down, and make ourselves available to others? We don't have to have it all together. It's all right to let our weakness show, to share our own doubts, to reveal who we really are. Evangelist Becky Pippert was profoundly changed when a student said to her, "The more you let me inside your life, the more impossible it became to keep the lid on Christianity. Even your admission of weakness drove me to him." What astonished Becky was that this student had seen her in all kinds of circumstances. "She had seen the real me," writes Becky, "—and it gave the gospel more power, not less. I had always thought I should cover up my doubts and problems, because if she knew me she wouldn't become a Christian. But the more open and transparent I was (even with my weaknesses), the more real Jesus Christ became to her."[11]

Seeing People for Who They Really Are

As he listened to his Father and to the woman, Jesus pushed through the racial, religious, cultural, and gender barriers and saw the deeper needs of the woman at the well. The woman had been married five times, and the man she was then living with was not her husband. The disciples would have taken one look at her and concluded, "That woman? Become a believer? No way!" Jesus came to the opposite conclusion. He knew the woman's lifestyle, her need for tenderness, her longing for acceptance, her need and hunger for God. He saw how hard she was trying to find the right thing in all the wrong places. He saw her potential to be a worshiper of the one true God, and he wanted to draw her deeper into conversation and relationship.

Are we accepting of others even when we cannot condone their actions or sins? Do we always see the tremendous worth and potential of the person before us, for whom Christ died and rose again? Do we see people the way Jesus sees them? The Holy Spirit wants us to recognize their needs, loneliness, longings, hopes, and dreams. He wants to give us the courage to reach out to them. He wants us to see that the neighbors next door or the people we meet at the market or on the street are not interruptions in our carefully controlled schedules, but people he is bringing before us by divine appointment.

Entering into the Lives of Those We Encounter

Jesus went beyond the deeds of the person to their deeper needs. He began talking to the woman about water, because she had come to draw water from the well. He then asked her questions about "living water" and answered her questions about true worship. He was a seed planter, sowing the gospel bit by bit, taking the risk to get beneath the surface of her life.

Are we so afraid of rejection or failure that we hold back and stay in our protected shells? Do we seek to enter the lives of our neighbors, friends, and acquaintances? An easy way to enter people's lives is to find simple ways to serve them—taking a meal to a sick neighbor or driving someone to the market or airport—asking questions along the way and taking time to affirm them by listening carefully. We too can be seed planters, being sacrificial with time, resources, and expertise, laying down our lives for others, counting on the Holy Spirit to draw nonbelievers to Jesus through us.

Welcoming Others into Our Lives

Jesus wanted the woman to know more about him, to know him as the giver of living water and the quencher of her thirst, to know him as her Messiah.

Do we welcome others into our lives? Do we invite them to join us in the places and events that give life to us—a close family event, weekly worship, or weekend recreation? Do we welcome people to join us in community worship where they may witness the reality of God (see chapter 10)? Sally Morgenthaler, in her book aptly titled *Worship Evangelism*, says that worship services can be conducted in such a Spirit-led and seeker-sensitive way that unbelievers feel invited into the presence of God. She points out that worship that edifies also witnesses, and worship that witnesses also edifies![12]

As mentioned in chapter 11, a loving fellowship of believers is the ultimate witness as people are drawn to Christ by the attractiveness of God's love incarnate in a human community. There was such love, freedom, joy, and power present in the witness of the first Christian fellowships that people were daily being saved and added to their numbers (Acts 2:47–48). How can we encourage that same spirit of witness today that leads to conversion and effective discipleship? Will we, by the Spirit's power, overcome our fears and the natural reticence of our individualistic culture and welcome people into our lives and communities?

Being Honest and Direct in Our Challenge

As he listened to the Holy Spirit, Jesus learned more of the woman's life than she had told him. He said to her, "Go, call your husband and come back." "I have no husband," she replied. Jesus affirmed her for speaking the truth and then let her know he knew all about her life (v. 16–18). Jesus was challenging the woman to be true about her own life, and then challenging her to learn the truth about himself (v. 26).

We too must be honest and direct in sharing the gospel. We must go beyond building bridges and caring relationships with non-Christians and eventually *cross* the bridges by challenging these people with the truth of Christ and encouraging them to receive him as their personal Lord and Savior. We must learn simple methods of communicating the gospel clearly, and be ready to share stories of how Jesus has changed our lives, give a few key Scripture verses that outline God's plan for salvation in Jesus Christ, and pray with those ready to commit their lives to Christ.

As we witness, the Spirit will remind us that the Lord has called us to not just make converts, but to make *disciples*. We will need to support and encourage new believers in the faith until they become members of local fellowships and are well on their way to maturity in Christ. God wants us to not only be spiritual obstetricians, delivering new spiritual babies into God's family, but also to be spiritual pediatricians, caring for new spiritual babies so that they can grow up spiritually strong and healthy.[13]

It is the Holy Spirit who empowers all aspects of spiritual encounters. The Holy Spirit leads us into divine appointments. He gives us strength for humility, helps us listen to the world around us, confers power to translate truth into words with meaning for the people we encounter, and gives us insights and words of knowledge that aid us in witnessing. The answer to effective witness is to be filled with the Holy Spirit!

Witnessing as a Way of Life

If we are to be faithful followers of Jesus Christ, his values must permeate our lives. His passion for the lost must become our passion. As we draw near to God through the spiritual disciplines, reaching out to others in loving service and witness will become natural to us. When we live as Jesus did, in his power and with his presence, others will be naturally drawn to us. Witnessing will not be a dreaded task to be ticked off our schedule of necessary Christian duties. Rather, sharing Jesus will become a true delight, and witnessing will become our natural lifestyle. Are we adequate for this lifestyle? Of course not! But remember, the Holy Spirit brings his power and ability to use our limited resources and abilities in his limitless ways.[14]

One of Doug's best friends has been set apart by God to regularly intercede for others, especially the lost. Doug was present when God released in this woman a gift of intercession, and he still gets goose bumps when he recalls the piercing scream she gave as she saw herself, in her mind's eye, standing in Christ's body and looking through Christ's eyes at lost souls walking the pathway into hell. She experienced Jesus' passion for the lost, his great unconditional love for all of those created in the image of God. Her heart was broken that day as she wept with Jesus for those who do not know him. She was drawn close to his loving heart as she prayed Spirit-guided prayers for her unsaved father. And her love for God grew deeper as she surrendered to his purpose for her life.

We won't all have such experiences of intercession—we won't all be spiritually gifted to be intercessors or evangelists. But for all of us, witnessing is to be a normal and natural Spirit-directed way of life. Witnessing is something we should be unable *not* to do. It is to flow out of us without our even realizing it. If our hearts are full of love for Jesus and his compassion for the lost, we are bound to witness naturally and spontaneously of him. God wants all people to be saved (1 Tim. 2:3–4) and none to perish but that all should come to repentance (2 Peter 3:9). Ed Silvoso challenges us to get with the heartbeat of God:

> Right now I want to invite you to lean your ear on God's chest and listen to His heartbeat.... Listen carefully and you will hear two sounds: none ... all. None to perish. All to come to repentance. Continue to listen until His heartbeat becomes your heartbeat, until you see all of your unsaved relatives, friends, neighbors, and coworkers in the monitor of your soul. As their names and faces come up, listen to God say, "None to perish ... all to come to repentance." Listen long enough ... stay put until God's love for the lost floods your heart, rises to your mind and completely renews it. Yes, catch God's heartbeat![15]

Social concern expressed in concrete actions is a critical part of witness and evangelism. As we enter into witness, the Holy Spirit will enlarge our vision to include the whole human family. World missions will be in our heart! But it is important that compassion, mercy, and witness start at home as we enter into the ministry of reconciliation (Gal. 3:28) by standing against racism, sexism, and other forms of social injustice and oppression. William Pannell reminds us that "professions to know God are empty if justice and mercy do not obtain between people.... spirituality is the shortest distance between two people. Reconciliation is at heart a matter of spirituality."[16]

Jesus is not only the best answer to the deepest needs of human beings today, he is the only answer, the only way back to God (John 14:6). He is the ultimate answer to our inner emptiness (John 6:35), purposelessness (John 8:12), fear of death (John 11:25–26), desire for inner peace (John 14:27), loneliness (Matt. 28:20), and the need for integrated truth in our thinking (John 14:6).[17] As we enter the spiritual discipline of witness, the Holy Spirit will help us to see the gospel as the power of God for the salvation of everyone who believes (Rom. 1:16). We will see lives being touched and transformed by the Spirit in his work of convicting and converting the lost to Christ. We will realize how great and powerful the gospel is for changing lives for eternity. And we will fall in love with Jesus over and over again as we witness and see him touching lives.

Entering In

Are you ready to let God reveal to you his heart and heartbeat for the lost? To have your passion for Jesus renewed and your compassion for the lost deepened? To live a Spirit-filled life that naturally overflows with excitement about Jesus? To witness more regularly in the power of the Holy Spirit? If so, then say yes to the Spirit's transforming work and expect to grow in the discipline of witness.

Right now:

Take a few moments to reflect on your current witness for Christ. When was the last time you prayed for the salvation of someone and, through clear words and loving actions, witnessed to the truth of Jesus? Pray:

> *Dear Lord, I confess my fears and struggles with witnessing. I want your heartbeat for the lost, and I ask for the power of the Holy Spirit to so fill me with holy boldness and loving sensitivity that I will be enabled to witness and share Jesus with others more openly and regularly. Grant me the blessed privilege and joy of leading people to faith in you. I am so glad to know you personally as my Lord and Savior, as the Way, the Truth, and the Life. In Jesus' name, Amen!*

In the coming days and weeks:

- Ask the Holy Spirit to lead you to two people who need to know Jesus as their friend. Pray that Jesus would meet these two people in their current circumstances and that the Spirit would open their eyes so they might see Jesus more clearly and be saved through faith in him.

❧ Spend time with the friends you are praying for. Enter into their lives; welcome them into your life. Plan one or two things to do with them this week. Ask questions and listen carefully; look for the Holy Spirit at work.

❧ Invite these friends individually to your home for a meal and share with them your testimony and your passion for Jesus. As the Spirit leads, challenge them with the gospel message so they can make a decision for Christ and become a disciple of Jesus if they want to. Pray with them to receive Christ. (For a sample prayer see note 1, chapter 1.)

❧ Ask God for "divine appointments" to share Jesus with people, even strangers. Carry with you a copy or two of an evangelism tool such as "The Four Spiritual Laws" or "Steps to Peace with God." Give them to people with whom you have had a chance to talk. As you sow this seed, pray for their salvation.

❧ Share your burden for the lost with a few other Christian friends who also have deep compassion for unbelievers. In a small group, pray for each other and for the salvation of each other's non-Christian friends, relatives, or acquaintances. In praying for one another, ask especially for the Spirit's power, joy, and love in your witness.

Epilogue
The Transformed Life

———————•◆•———————

In the preceding chapters, we have explained how you can continually connect with the power of the Holy Spirit through the disciplines of the Holy Spirit, for the purpose of being transformed into the likeness of Jesus Christ.

God purposes that we "be conformed to the likeness of his Son" (Rom. 8:29). He wants us to walk in the Spirit, day by day, year after year, for a lifetime, to be built up "until we all reach unity in the faith and in the knowledge of the Son of God and become mature, attaining to the whole measure of the fullness of Christ" (Eph. 4:13, 15).

Our deepest longing can be met only through relationship with Jesus, through conformity of our hearts and minds to his life and character. Jesus Christ is the great "Good News." He is the answer to the deepest cries of the human heart—the cry for purpose in an empty existence, the cry for love and acceptance in an age of selfishness, the cry for freedom when human oppression abounds on every side. All of our human cries are at bottom a cry for God, and Jesus is the answer because he alone, by his living presence among us, has the power to change us.[1] Becoming more like Jesus is becoming our true selves. The greatest sign and wonder the world can see is the transformation of people into his likeness.

Living the Spirit-filled Life

This journey into true spirituality requires the transforming power of the Holy Spirit. Our part is to yield to the power and influence of the Holy Spirit through the spiritual disciplines, giving him time and space to speak to us and guide us, to fill us and empower us, to turn us around and transform us. Through the spiritual disciplines, *the Spirit of God is working out the will of God to make the children of God like the Son of God.* The disciplines of the Spirit are the God-given means we are to use in our Spirit-filled pursuit of growing into the heart of God, into the likeness of Jesus.

Jesus promised his followers that they would have powerful, loving, and fruitful lives as the result of being filled with the Holy Spirit; and he was true to his word. At Pentecost, when the Spirit came, the love and power of God so overwhelmed and transformed the timid disciples that nothing could stop them. Filled with the Spirit, they initiated the greatest spiritual revolution the world has ever known. Within three centuries, even the mighty Roman Empire yielded to the power of the gospel of Jesus Christ. Out they went, rejoicing, praising, surrendering, serving, and witnessing—the love of Christ constraining them.

The same is to be true for us. We are to be filled with the fullness of God, overwhelmed with the length and breadth and height and depth of the love of Christ, so that we too speak of the greatness of God (Eph. 3:18–19; Acts 2:11). We are to be transformed by our experience of God—to know the peace that passes understanding, to have the love which surpasses knowledge, to know the fullness of his joy—to have the quality of peace, love, and joy that the world can neither give nor take away.

Experiencing God's Embrace

Several times in the book of Acts we read that the Spirit "fell" on a group of people (Acts 10:44; 11:15 NRSV). In other passages in the New Testament the same word, *epipipto,* is used in the context of an affectionate embrace. For example, in Luke 15:20, the father of the prodigal son "threw his arms around him"—"fell on his neck" (KJV), "embraced him" (RSV)—when the son returned home. The falling of the Holy Spirit is like a divine embrace of love. When we are embraced by the Spirit, our spirits leap within us, crying "Abba! Father!" We experience within our hearts the amazing love of God.

When the Holy Spirit throws his arms around you in this way, it's like being a small child walking along holding your father's hand. All is well. You are happy and secure in your father's presence. You know your father loves you. Then, suddenly, your father startles you by reaching down, sweeping you up into his arms, hugging you tightly, kissing you on the cheek, and whispering, "I love you so much!" And then, holding you up like a trophy at arm's length, he looks into your face and says with all his heart, "I am so glad you are mine."

When the Holy Spirit embraces us like this, we are stunned. We don't know whether to cry or shout or fall down or laugh or run about. The fuses of love are so overloaded they almost blow out. The subconscious doubts that pop up from time to time are gone, replaced by utter and indestructible assurance that God is real and that Jesus lives and that we are loved, and that to be saved is the greatest thing in the world. And as we walk on down the street, we can scarcely contain ourselves. We want to cry out and sing, "This is my Father's world."[2]

When we are filled with the Holy Spirit, when God throws his arms around us, we enter into the most passionate love affair of life.

Growing in God

Growth in God requires passion, courage, persistence, patience, time, and self-discipline. Paul wrote to Timothy to remind him to "fan into flame the gift of God," which is the Spirit himself. "For God did not give us a spirit of timidity, but a spirit of power, of love and of self-discipline" (2 Tim. 1:6–7). To those filled with the Holy Spirit, God gives power, love, *and self-discipline*. As we said at the beginning of this book, no one drifts casually into vital spirituality!

We are, by and large, busy people, living in a fast-paced culture, who define ourselves by our productivity and accomplishments. The temptation is always present to avoid prayer, study, worship, and other spiritual practices. "There just isn't enough time!" we insist. It is so easy to make excuses, to take the easy way out, to put other things before growth in God—victims of our age and culture. But this is nonsense!

Jesus was busy, but he was never frantic. In Mark, "immediately" describes the transition from one event in Jesus' life to the next. Jesus ministered all day and into the night, and then got up before dawn to pray. He often prayed through the night. He was so tired one day that he slept through a storm. Crowds pressed upon him, everyone wanted time with him. Yet he was continually at peace, resting in the easy yoke of relationship to his Father.

How can you grow in God? By practicing the spiritual disciplines! "Work out your salvation with fear and trembling," says Paul (Phil. 2:12). Through the disciplines, busy people can be changed into godly people. The spiritual disciplines aren't just for people with lots of spare time. They are disciplines by which busy people become more like Jesus. They are the means God uses to speak to us, to draw us close to himself, to help us establish priorities, to discover what must be pruned away, to help us stay in a centered place no matter what demands are being made upon us.[3] They aren't an added burden, but the pathway to freedom. We will continue to be busy, but if we allow our jobs, hobbies, and ministries to keep us from connecting with the Spirit through the disciplines, we will be captured by the world's agenda, squeezed, as Paul says, into the world's mold.

How can you persevere in the disciplines of the Spirit? By the power of the Holy Spirit! "Work out your own salvation," says Paul, "for it is God who works in you to will and to act according to his good purpose" (Phil. 2:13). "He who began a good work in you will carry it on to completion until the day of Christ Jesus" (Phil. 1:6). The Holy Spirit creates the hunger and thirst for God in us, producing within us the desire and the power for the transformed life. The Holy Spirit keeps the fire of discipline going in your daily life. When you are feeling lazy, discouraged, distracted, disappointed, or absent from God, the Spirit prompts you to begin again, pray again, worship again, serve again. Self-control is part of the fruit of the Spirit's work in your life (Gal. 5:23). The Spirit is faithful to help each of us persevere to the end in those things which will make us like Christ.

Growing in God is a great adventure! It is neither our work nor the Spirit's work alone, but our responding to and cooperating with the Holy Spirit who initiates and supports our spiritual growth. Paul says, "I labor, struggling with all his energy, which so powerfully works in me" (Col. 1:29). The Greek word for "labor," from which we get our English word "agonize," suggests struggling and striving until one is weary. We grow in God by means of our own labor, but we labor according to the energy of the Holy Spirit at work in us. Where the Spirit is at work there is always the possibility for courageous and self-disciplined living beyond what might be expected. "Everything is possible for him who believes" (Mark 9:23).

We are to be on the journey toward true spirituality in a serious way—to "run the race that is set before us" (Heb. 12:1) and to finish well (2 Tim. 4:7). God is calling us to be his light, leaven, salt. He invites us to a kingdom banquet. By responding, "Hey, God, I'm coming," we are committing to the disciplines and to being available to shaping and empowerment by the Holy Spirit for God's purposes. We are to be rivers of living water, workers of signs and wonders; but even more, we are to be the signs and wonders themselves. In our intimacy with him, our submission and humility before him, our service and availability to others in his name, we are to light up the sky and reflect the brightness of Christ's glory.

The challenge before you is to grow into the heart of God. The means—the disciplines of the Holy Spirit—are at hand. The rewards are the abundant life promised by Jesus, walking in the Spirit day by day, year after year, for a lifetime, as we grow in maturity in Christ and are transformed into the likeness of Jesus.

What wonderful riches! May God bless you on your journey into true spirituality.

Notes

Part I—Connecting to the Power of the Holy Spirit

Chapter 1: The Power of the Holy Spirit

1. For those of you reading this book who may be in a similar situation—either never having asked Jesus to be your Lord and Savior or unsure if you have said so from your heart—please take a few minutes to review the following Scriptures and pray, asking God to take control of your life. This is the first crucial step in the most exciting adventure anyone can undertake.

a. Romans 3:23: For all have sinned and fall short of the glory of God.

b. Romans 6:23: For the wages of sin is death, but the gift of God is eternal life in Christ Jesus our Lord.

c. Romans 5:8: But God demonstrates his own love for us in this: While we were still sinners, Christ died for us.

d. Romans 10:9–10: That if you confess with your mouth, "Jesus is Lord," and believe in your heart that God raised him from the dead, you will be saved. For it is with your heart that you believe and are justified, and it is with your mouth that you confess and are saved.

e. Romans 10:13: For, "Everyone who calls on the name of the Lord will be saved."

[Sample prayer] Dear Lord Jesus, I admit that I am a sinner and lost without you. Thank you for dying on the cross for my sins and for rising from the dead so that I can enter new and eternal life with you. I now accept you into my heart as my personal Lord and Savior. I ask you to take control of my life from now on and to fill me with your Holy Spirit so that I can live as a true Christian each day of my life. Thank you, Jesus. Amen.

2. Henri Nouwen, *The Return of the Prodigal Son* (New York: Image Books, 1994), 43–44.

3. From C. S. Lewis, *Mere Christianity*, quoted in Richard Foster, *Devotional Classics* (San Francisco: HarperCollins, 1993), 8.

4. Thomas Merton, "Thoughts in Solitude," quoted in Don Postema, *Space for God* (Grand Rapids: CRC Press, 1983), 60.

5. Henry T. Blackaby and Claude V. King, *Experiencing God* (Nashville: Lifeway Press, 1990), 24.

6. See, for example, Campus Crusade's little booklet "Have You Made the Wonderful Discovery of the Spirit-Filled Life?" published by Campus Crusade for Christ International, Arrowhead Springs, Calif., 1966.

Chapter 2: The Disciplines of the Holy Spirit

1. Dallas Willard, *The Spirit of the Disciplines* (San Francisco: Harper & Row, 1988), ix.

2. J. I. Packer, *Rediscovering Holiness* (Ann Arbor, Mich.: Servant, 1992), 237–38.

Part II—Drawing Near to God: Disciplines of Solitude

Chapter 3: Solitude and Silence

1. Henri Nouwen, *Making All Things New* (San Francisco: Harper & Row, 1981), 69.

2. Richard Foster, *Prayer, Finding the Heart's True Home* (San Francisco: HarperSanFrancisco, 1992), 1.

3. Julian of Norwich, *Showings* (New York: Paulist Press, 1978), 300.

4. Frank C. Laubach, *Letters by a Modern Mystic* (New York: New Readers Press, 1955), 11, 19.

5. Henri Nouwen, *In the Name of Jesus* (New York: Crossroad, 1989), 71.

6. Ibid., 29–30.

7. A. W. Tozer, *That Incredible Christian* (Beaverlodge, Alberta: Horizon House, 1977), 122, 124.

Chapter 4: Listening and Guidance

1. Henri Nouwen, *Making All Things New* (San Francisco: Harper & Row, 1981), 54.

2. G. Campbell Morgan, *God's Perfect Will* (Grand Rapids: Baker, 1978), 157.

3. Richard Foster, *Celebration of Discipline* (San Francisco: Harper & Row, 1978), 150.

4. Ibid.

5. See, for example, Frank Laubach, "Letters by a Modern Mystic" and "Game with Minutes" in *Frank Laubach, Man of Prayer, The Heritage Collection* (Syracuse, N.Y.: New Reader's Press, Laubach Literacy International, 1990), 17–48, 191–207.

6. Henry T. Blackaby and Claude V. King, *Experiencing God* (Nashville: Lifeway Press, 1990), 33.

7. Ibid., 34.

8. F. B. Meyer, *The Secret of Guidance* (Chicago: Moody Press, 1896), 14, 16.

Chapter 5: Prayer and Intercession

1. Randall D. Roth, *Prayer Powerpoints* (Wheaton: Victor, 1995), 19.

2. Julian of Norwich, *Revelations of Divine Love*, translated into modern English by Clifton Wolters (London: Penguin, 1966), 128.

3. E. M. Bounds, *Power Through Prayer* (Grand Rapids: Zondervan, 1962), 12.

4. Wesley Duewel, *Touch the World Through Prayer* (Grand Rapids: Zondervan, 1986), 45.

5. Roth, *Prayer Powerpoints*, 12.

6. Ibid., 23.

7. Many excellent books are available on healing prayer. See Francis MacNutt, *Healing* (Notre Dame, Ind.: Ave Maria, 1974); Mike Flynn and Doug Gregg, *Inner Healing* (Downers Grove: InterVarsity Press, 1993); Thomas White, *The Believer's Guide to Spiritual Warfare* (Ann Arbor, Mich.: Servant/Vine, 1990); Charles H. Kraft, *Deep Wounds, Deep Healing* (Ann Arbor, Mich.: Servant, 1993); David Seamands, *Healing of Memories* (Wheaton: Victor, 1985); John and Mark Sandford, *Deliverance and Inner Healing* (Grand Rapids: Chosen, 1992); Neil Anderson, *Living Free in Christ* (Ventura, Calif.: Regal, 1993).

8. Richard Foster, *Prayer, Finding the Heart's True Home* (San Francisco: HarperCollins, 1992), 240–41.

9. Ibid., 119.

10. Sheldon D. Gordon, *Quiet Talks on Prayer* (Grand Rapids: Revell, 1967), 11.

Chapter 6: Study and Meditation

1. John Wesley, *Fifty Three Sermons* (Nashville: Abingdon, 1745, 1983), 13.

2. John Rea, *The Layman's Commentary on the Holy Spirit* (Plainfield, N.J.: Logos International, 1974), 198–99.

3. A. W. Tozer, *That Incredible Christian* (Harrisburg, Penn.: Christian, 1964), 82.

4. See, for example, *The One Year Bible* (Wheaton: Tyndale, 1986).

5. For example, see G. Fee and D. Stuart, *How to Read the Bible for All Its Worth*, 2d ed. (Grand Rapids: Zondervan, 1993) and R. C. Sproul, *Knowing Scripture* (Downers Grove: InterVarsity Press, 1977). The sixty-six books of the Protestant Bible were originally written in three languages: Hebrew (most of the Old Testament), Aramaic (a sister language to Hebrew used in half of Daniel and two passages in Ezra), and Greek (all of the New Testament). Since most of us are not professional theologians and therefore do not know the original languages, we need to have good English translations of the Bible for our study of God's Word so that the original meanings of the text will not be lost. Good and accurate translations of the Bible include the New International Version (NIV), the New Revised Standard Version (NRSV), the Good News Bible (GNB), and the New American Standard Bible (NASB). A study Bible edition of any of these translations will be a great help for the study of God's Word. There are many other helpful Bible study tools, such as a Bible dictionary, handbook, concordance, and commentaries. Here are some examples:

   a. A one-volume Bible commentary on the whole Bible: See the *New Bible Commentary*, 21st *Century Edition*, G. J. Wenham, J. A. Motyer, D. A. Carson, R. T. France, eds. (Downers Grove: InterVarsity Press, 1994).

   b. Commentary sets or commentaries on each book of the Bible: The Expositor's Bible Commentary (12 volumes) published by Zondervan can be particularly helpful in serious

Bible study. Other recommendations, especially for individual commentaries on each book of the Bible, can be found in Fee and Stuart's (1993) book cited above. They include William Barclay's Daily Study Bible covering the whole New Testament in 17 volumes, The New International Commentary series as well as the Tyndale Old Testament Commentaries.

c. Bible dictionary and Bible handbook: These tools are used for background information and definitions. See the *New Bible Dictionary*, 2d edition, J. D. Douglas, F. F. Bruce, J. U. Packer, N. Hillyer, D. Guthrie, A. R. Millard, and D. J. Wiseman, eds. (Downers Grove: InterVarsity Press, 1982).

d. Systematic theology textbooks: A good text on systematic theology written for the layperson is *Foundations of the Christian Faith* by James Montgomery Boice (Downers Grove: InterVarsity Press, 1986). A more recent text written for students and Christians in general is *Systematic Theology: An Introduction to Biblical Doctrine* by Wayne Grudem (Grand Rapids: Zondervan, 1994).

e. A concordance: For example, Strong's Concordance lists all relevant passages in the Bible on significant words. A helpful tool for doing specific word studies of particular words in the Bible covering both Old and New Testaments is the book *An Expository Dictionary of Biblical Words* by W. E. Vine, Merrill F. Unger, and William White, Jr. (Nashville: Thomas Nelson, 1984).

f. Bible study booklets/series: A guided study through specific books of the Bible (e.g. Irving Jensen's Bible self-study guides published by Moody Press) can deepen a Christian's understanding of God's Word.

6. Donald S. Whitney, *Spiritual Disciplines for the Christian Life* (Colorado Springs: Navpress, 1991), 70–72.

7. J. Adams, *Ready to Restore: The Layman's Guide to Christian Counseling* (Grand Rapids: Baker, 1981), 64–65.

8. Ideas drawn from Cathy Schaller, *Further Up and Further In—An Eight-Week Journey Towards Intimacy with God*, section on *lectio divina*, published by the author, 1995, available from the author at Fuller Theological Seminary, Pasadena, CA.

9. St. Ignatius, *The Spiritual Exercises of St. Ignatius* (New York: Image, Doubleday, 1964).

10. Thanks to the Navigators for this helpful illustration.

Part III — Yielding to God: Disciplines of Surrender

Chapter 7: Repentance and Confession

1. Charles G. Finney, *An Autobiography* (London: Salvation Army Book Department, 1868), 10–13.

2. Ibid., 13–25.

3. Oswald Chambers, *The Shadow of an Agony* (Fort Washington, Penn.: Christian Literature Crusade, 1934), 121.

4. Eugene Peterson, *Praying with Jesus* (San Francisco: HarperSanFrancisco, 1993), selection for Nov. 1.

5. J. I. Packer, *Rediscovering Holiness* (Ann Arbor, Mich.: Servant, 1992), 122–24.

6. Ibid., 147.

7. Henri Nouwen, *In the Name of Jesus* (New York: Crossroad, 1989), 46.

8. William Barclay, *The Letters to the Corinthians*, revised edition (Philadelphia: Westminster, 1975), 226–27.

9. Quoted in Maxie Dunnam, *The Workbook on Spiritual Disciplines* (Nashville: The Upper Room, 1984), 69.

10. *Los Angeles Times*, Monday, 19 June 1995, 1, 15. See John Dawson, *Healing America's Wounds* (Ventura, Calif.: Regal, 1994).

11. From a tape-recorded talk, quoted in David Watson, *One in the Spirit* (London: Hodder and Stoughton, 1973), 41.

12. Packer, *Holiness*, 144.

Chapter 8: Yielding and Submission

1. Oswald Chambers, *Oswald Chambers—The Best from All His Books* (Nashville: Thomas Nelson, 1987), 346.

2. C. S. Lewis, *Mere Christianity* (New York: Macmillan, 1952), 167.

3. François Fénelon, in Foster and Smith, *Devotional Classics* (San Francisco: HarperSanFrancisco, 1990), 47.

4. David Watson, *One in the Spirit* (London: Hodder and Stoughton, 1973), 61–64.

5. Quoted in Richard Foster, *Prayer, Finding the Heart's True Home* (San Francisco: HarperSanFrancisco, 1992), 47.

6. Lewis B. Smedes, *Mere Morality* (Grand Rapids: Eerdmans, 1983), 78.

7. J. I. Packer, *Rediscovering Holiness* (Ann Arbor, Mich.: Servant, 1992), 120.

8. Raphael Brown, trans., *The Little Flowers of St. Francis* (Garden City, N.Y.: Image, Doubleday, 1958). See Douglas H. Gregg, "The Little Flowers of St. Francis," in Frank N. Magill and Ian P. McGreal, eds., *Christian Spirituality* (San Francisco: Harper and Row, 1988), 144–48.

9. Thomas Kelly, *Testament of Devotion* (San Francisco: HarperSanFrancisco, 1992), 54.

10. Brown, *Little Flowers*, 44.

11. Therese of Lisieux, *The Story of a Soul*, translated by John Beevers (New York: Image, 1989).

12. Oswald Chambers, *God's Workmanship* (Fort Washington, Penn.: Christian Literature Crusade, 1953), 29.

13. Andrew Murray, *Absolute Surrender* (Springdale, Penn.: Whitaker, 1981), 8.

14. Judson W. Van de Venter, "I Surrender All," vv. 3–4, *Hymns for the Family of God* (Nashville: Paragon, 1976), 408.

Chapter 9: Fasting

1. Arthur Wallis, *God's Chosen Fast* (Fort Washington, Penn.: Christian Literature Crusade, 1968), 25–26.

2. David R. Smith, *Fasting: A Neglected Discipline* (Fort Washington, Penn.: Christian Literature Crusade, 1954), 46–47.

3. Donald S. Whitney, *Spiritual Disciplines for the Christian Life* (Colorado Springs: Navpress, 1991), 157. Many ideas in this section are supported by Whitney's helpful chapter on fasting, especially pp. 156–70.

4. Jonathan Edwards, ed., *The Life and Diary of David Brainerd* (Chicago: Moody Press, 1949), 88.

5. Dietrich Bonhoeffer, *The Cost of Discipleship* (New York: Collier, 1963), 188–89.

6. Whitney, *Disciplines*, 162.

7. Ibid., 153–54.

8. Bill Bright, *The Coming Revival: America's Call to Fast, Pray, and "Seek God's Face"* (Orlando: New Life, 1995), 29.

9. See Ibid., 127–52 for helpful suggestions on preparing for and beginning a fast.

10. Derek Kamemoto, from class paper on fasting written for Introduction to Christian Spirituality, taught by Dr. Gregg during summer term, 1995.

11. Oswald Chambers, *The Psychology of Redemption* (Fort Washington, Penn.: Christian Literature Crusade, 1930), 58.

12. Quoted in Randall D. Roth, *Prayer Powerpoints* (Wheaton: Victor, 1995), 204.

Chapter 10: Worship

1. A. W. Tozer, *That Incredible Christian* (Harrisburg, Penn.: Christian, 1964), 126.

2. Our appreciation to colleague Cathy Schaller, Associate Director in the Office of Christian Community at Fuller Seminary, for sparking in us several ideas contained in this chapter and her permission to develop them in our own way.

3. John Piper, *Desiring God* (Portland, Ore.: Multnomah, 1986), 61–62, 65.

4. Ibid., 66.

5. Julian of Norwich, *Revelations of Divine Love*, translated by Clifton Wolters (London: Penguin, 1966), 70–71.

6. John R. W. Stott, *Baptism and Fullness: The Work of the Holy Spirit Today* (Downers Grove: InterVarsity Press, 1975), 57–58.

7. David A. Hubbard, *The Holy Spirit in Today's World* (Waco: Word, 1973), 110.

8. C. S. Lewis, *Reflections on the Psalms* (New York: Harcourt Brace Jovanovich, 1964), 90–97.

9. Ibid.

10. David Watson, *One in the Spirit* (London: Hodder and Stoughton, 1973), 35–36.

11. For a more complete account of this story, see Mike Flynn and Doug Greg, *Inner Healing—A Handbook for Helping Yourself and Others* (Downers Grove: InterVarsity Press, 1993), 178–80.

12. Frances R. Havergal, "Take My Life and Let It Be," Psalter Hymnal, #462.

Part IV—Reaching Out to Others: Disciplines of Service

Chapter 11: Fellowship

1. J. I. Packer, *God's Words: Studies of Key Bible Themes* (Downers Grove: InterVarsity Press, 1981), 195.

2. David Watson, *Called and Committed: World-Changing Discipleship* (Wheaton: Harold Shaw, 1982), 17

3. Ibid., 30.

4. Donald P. McNeill, Douglas A. Morrison, and Henri J. M. Nouwen, *Compassion—A Reflection on the Christian Life* (Garden City, N.Y.: Image, Doubleday, 1982), 51.

5. Ron Sider, *Rich Christians in an Age of Hunger* (Downers Grove: InterVarsity Press, 1977), 180.

6. C. S. Lewis, *The Screwtape Letters* (Great Britain: Collins, Fontana, 1942), 92–93.

7. Darrell Johnson, *Glendale Presbyterian Church Family News* (Glendale, Calif.: Glendale Presbyterian Church, March 1996), 1.

8. See Rich Lamb's helpful chapter "Community After College" in *Following Jesus in the Real World* (Downers Grove: InterVarsity Press, 1995), 88–113.

9. Dietrich Bonhoeffer, *Life Together* (New York: Harper and Row, 1954), 24–25.

10. Ibid., 23.

11. Ibid.

12. Andrew Murray, *Absolute Surrender* (Springdale, Penn.: Whitaker, 1981), 16.

Chapter 12: Simplicity

1. J. B. Phillips, *The Young Church in Action* (New York: Macmillan, 1955), vii.

2. The brief definitions for the spiritual gifts of giving, mercy, hospitality, and voluntary poverty are drawn from C. Peter Wagner, *Your Spiritual Gifts Can Help Your Church Grow* (Ventura, Calif.: Regal, 1994), 229–33.

3. Richard J. Foster, *Freedom of Simplicity* (San Francisco: Harper and Row, 1981), 45–46.

4. G. K. Chesterton, *St. Francis of Assisi* (Garden City, N.Y.: Image, Doubleday, 1957), 116. See Douglas H. Gregg, "St. Francis of Assisi," in *Christian Spirituality—The Essential Guide to the Most Influential Spiritual Writings of the Christian Tradition,* Frank Magill and Ian McGreal, eds., (San Francisco: Harper and Row, 1988), 491–95.

5. J. Hudson Taylor, *Hudson Taylor* (Minneapolis: Bethany, n.d.), 20.

6. Richard J. Foster, *Celebration of Discipline* (San Francisco: Harper and Row, 1978), 70–71.

7. Taylor, *Taylor,* 21.

8. Maxie Dunnam, *The Workbook on Spiritual Disciplines* (Nashville: The Upper Room, 1984), 139.

9. Ibid., 140–41.

10. Kari Brodin, Fuller Seminary Lenten Devotional, 1996.

11. Nancy Thomas, "Plain Speech for Intelligent People," *The Semi* (publication of Fuller Seminary's Office of Student Services, March 25, 1996), 2, 6.

Chapter 13: Service

1. E. Stanley Jones, *The Unshakable Kingdom* (Nashville: Abingdon, 1972), 54.

2. Harry Verploegh, *Signposts: A Collection of Sayings from A. W. Tozer* (Wheaton: Victor, 1988), 183.

3. C. Peter Wagner, *Your Spiritual Gifts Can Help Your Church Grow* (Ventura, Calif.: 1994), 109–26.

4. There are many books and materials available on the gifts of the Holy Spirit. In addition to Wagner, cited above, we recommend J. Robert Clinton, *Spiritual Gifts—A Self-Study or Group Study Manual* (Beaverlodge, Alberta: Horizon House, 1985).

5. Donald P. McNeill, Douglas A. Morrison, and Henri J. M. Nouwen, *Compassion—A Reflection on the Christian Life* (Garden City, N.Y.: Image, Doubleday, 1983), 27–28.

6. We acknowledge the influence of our pastor friend and colleague Darrell W. Johnson in his sermon "Following the King Whose Scepter is a Towel, " preached at Glendale Presbyterian Church, February 25, 1996.

7. Maxie Dunham, *The Workbook on Spiritual Disciplines* (Nashville: The Upper Room, 1984), 109.

8. McNeill, Morrison, and Nouwen, *Compassion,* 4.

9. Ibid., 29.

10. Maxie Dunham, *Alive in Christ* (Nashville: Abingdon, 1982), 150.

11. Donald S. Whitney, *Spiritual Disciplines for the Christian Life* (Colorado Springs: Navpress, 1991), 116.

12. Norman Grubb, *Rees Howells—Intercessor* (Fort Washington, Penn.: Christian Literature Crusade, 1952, 1980), 110–11.

13. See Robert K. Greenleaf, *Servant Leadership* (New York: Paulist, 1977), 9–39.

14. From "Letters on Modern Atheism," quoted in *Sojourners Magazine*, Dec. 1981, 17.

15. Jeremy Taylor, quoted in *Devotional Classics*, Richard J. Foster and James Bryan Smith, eds., (San Francisco: HarperSanFrancisco, 1993), 270.

16. Grubb, *Intercessor*, 46.

17. Ibid., 46–47.

18. Ibid., 47.

19. Jones, *Kingdom*, 54.

Chapter 14: Witness

1. Richard J. Foster and James Bryan Smith, "Sadu Sundar Singh: Sharing the Joy with Others," *Devotional Classics* (San Francisco: HarperSanFrancisco, 1994), 308–13.

2. J. I. Packer, *Evangelism and the Sovereignty of God* (Downers Grove: InterVarsity Press, 1979), 37–57.

3. Paul Little, *How to Give Away Your Faith* (Downers Grove: InterVarsity Press, 1988), 190.

4. D. Martyn Lloyd-Jones, *Joy Unspeakable* (Wheaton: Harold Shaw, 1984), 75.

5. David Watson, *One in the Spirit* (London: Hodder and Stoughton, 1973), 70–71.

6. C. Peter Wagner, *On the Crest of the Wave: Becoming a World Christian* (Ventura, Calif.: Regal, 1983), 67.

7. John Wimber with Kevin Springer, *Power Evangelism* (San Francisco: Harper and Row, 1986), 51.

8. Henry T. Blackaby and Claude V. King, *Experiencing God* (Nashville: Lifeway Press, 1990), 26.

9. Ibid.

10. J. Mack Stiles, *Speaking of Jesus* (Downers Grove: InterVarsity Press, 1995), 71–78. See also Don Dunkerley, *Healing Evangelism* (Grand Rapids: Chosen, 1995).

11. Rebecca Manley Pippert, *Out of the Saltshaker and into the World* (Downers Grove: InterVarsity Press, 1979), 29–30.

12. Sally Morganthaler, *Worship Evangelism* (Grand Rapids: Zondervan, 1995).

13. See Bill Hybels and Mark Mittelberg, *Becoming a Contagious Christian* (Grand Rapids: Zondervan, 1994); Win Arn and Charles Arn, *The Master's Plan for Making Disciples* (Pasadena: Church Growth, 1982); Francis M. Cosgrove, Jr., *Essentials of Discipleship* (Colorado Springs: NavPress, 1980), Gary W. Kuhne, *The Dynamics of Personal Follow-up* (Grand Rapids: Zondervan, 1976).

14. Pippert, *Saltshaker*, 102, 104.

15. Ed Silvoso, *That None Should Perish* (Ventura, Calif.: Regal, 1994), 96.

16. William Pannell, *The Coming Race Wars? A Cry for Reconciliation* (Grand Rapids: Zondervan, 1993), 140.

17. Paul Little, *Give Away*, 134–35.

Epilogue: The Transformed Life

1. David Watson, *Called and Committed* (Wheaton: Harold Shaw, 1982), 2.

2. This idea originates with Thomas Goodwin, a brilliant Puritan scholar of three hundred years ago, as referred to in D. Martyn Lloyd-Jones, *Joy Unspeakable* (Wheaton: Harold Shaw, 1984), 95–96.

3. Donald S. Whitney, *Spiritual Disciplines for the Christian Life* (Colorado Springs: NavPress, 1991), 225–27.

We want to hear from you. Please send your comments about this book to us in care of the address below. Thank you.

ZondervanPublishingHouse
Grand Rapids, Michigan 49530
http://www.zondervan.com